THE SHAREPOINT©
BUSINESS
ANALYST GUIDE

MATTHEW J. BAILEY, MCT

ISBN: **9781973174479**

DEDICATION & ACKNOWLEDGMENTS

I would like to dedicate this book to so many of the people who have helped me learn SharePoint and given me speaking opportunities over the years including: Vlad Catrinescu, Paul Choquette, Susan Lennon, Eric Harlan, Nikkia Carter, Dan Usher, Dennis Hassenfang, Mark Q. Jones, Shadeed Eleazer, Melissa Hubbard, Beau Cameron, Tim Ferro and others.

I would also like to dedicate this book to anyone who is reinventing themselves or investing in their job skills in hopes of moving forward in their career.

FORWARD

Whether you are just evaluating SharePoint, or you are a seasoned professional, you have probably already heard that most SharePoint deployments are not considered successful despite how powerful and versatile SharePoint is. One of the main reason that projects fail, is that no one actually talks to the users and stakeholders before getting the technical people in to install and customize the platform.

The reason I know is that back in 2014 when I first met Matthew, I was one of those purely technical people, specializing in the IT pro side of SharePoint. Every time I was assigned on a project, I hoped that there was a business analyst on the project that met the users, and had documented all the requirements and features that this organization planned to get out of SharePoint. While this was the case most of the time, I have worked on multiple projects with the *"If we build it they will come"* mentality, and those are exactly the projects that unfortunately ended in the statistic above.

While ten years ago, users would still use this failed deployment, the availability of hundreds, if not thousands of consumer tools for every business need has completely changed the landscape of IT. Business Users can now simply go on the internet, buy the tools they need for only a few dollars per user per month, without even asking IT for permission. This doesn't only lead to a waste of money and resources for the company, but also to potential security problems by having important and confidential information across the internet. Whatever your role is in the IT team today, you need to make users your #1 priority, and you need to make sure to involve them in every new solution that you implement.

As a business analyst with more than 10 years of experience in SharePoint, Matthew has helped thousands of people like myself with how to properly approach a SharePoint project, gather the right requirements, and deliver more successful SharePoint projects that are loved by users.

Whether you are an IT Professional, Developer or already a Business Analyst, this book will give you the tools and knowledge you need to deliver successful SharePoint projects for your organization and your clients.

Vlad Catrinescu
SharePoint Consultant and Author
5-time Microsoft MVP

Vlad Catrinescu

President & SharePoint Consultant
vNext Solutions

w: vnext.solutions   e: vlad@vnext.solutions

    amazon Author Central

TABLE OF CONTENTS

WHO SHOULD READ THIS BOOK & ASSUMPTIONS

Take what you can use and leave the rest.

This book was written in sections that should allow you to find specific pieces of information that you need at the time you need it for your SharePoint projects. Although reading it from front to back is great, I understand that most people are short on time and have a lot of demands made upon them. That being said, feel free to read the sections that apply to the needs of your situation and leave the rest for another time when you need it.

The audience for this book is anyone who is interested or working on SharePoint projects from beginners to mid-level users. It is also for anyone looking for time saving information, templates and great ideas on how to make your SharePoint projects a success.

THIS BOOK IS AVAILABLE IN A WORD OR PDF FORMAT WITH PROOF OF PURCHASE IF YOU ARE HAVING ISSUES WITH READING OR USING THE BOOK.

PLEASE VISIT
HTTP://WWW.MATTHEWJBAILEY.COM/SHAREPOINT-BUSINESS-ANALYST/
TO REQUEST THE FILES.

1. THE SHAREPOINT BUSINESS ANALYST

What is a SharePoint Business Analyst?

The term "SharePoint Business Analyst" has been thrown around quite a bit in the industry over the years. Due to their being a lack of a name for someone who works with SharePoint and performs multiple job roles, the SharePoint Business Analyst has also become the "catch all" for people in this category. A few formal definitions of what the business analyst job role are as follows:

A business analyst works as a liaison among stakeholders to elicit, analyze, communicate and validate requirements for changes to business processes, policies and information systems. The business analyst understands business problems and opportunities in the context of the requirements, and recommends solutions that enable the organization to achieve its goals." - www.iiba.org

"Business analysis is the practice of enabling change in an enterprise by defining needs and recommending solutions that deliver value to stakeholders. Business analysis enables an enterprise to articulate needs and the rationale for change, and to design and describe solutions that can deliver value." – BABOK® Guide V3

In reality however, the job role of the SharePoint Business Analyst can really be a number of things including:

- Does a bit of everything with SharePoint
- Meets with stakeholders / conducts requirement gathering sessions, creates clear agendas and realistically obtains answers needed
- Takes notes, meeting minutes, keeps everyone up to date to continually prevent issues from occurring
- Project management
- Creates solutions to business problems using SharePoint
- Understand usability / delivers and ensures satisfactory delivery of projects
- Creates requirements, performs testing, discusses governance
- Is a power user and might build no-code solutions or lightweight projects
- Is the "go to" person in their organization for SharePoint help or training
- Doesn't quite fit in anywhere else in the world of SharePoint, yet is part of most of SharePoint
- Does the job of five people, but the company that hired you has given you this title so they can pay you far less than what it would cost to hire those five people – *(a little humor added to make you smile…)*

To summarize, the best way to know specifically what skills you should learn to become a

SharePoint business analyst is to search job postings on the internet with that title in the area you live, talk with recruiters or network with others on tech community websites and at user groups. Since each job will vary a bit you should take at least a little time to make sure you are focusing on the right skill set to learn so you will have a good chance of landing a job as a SharePoint business analyst.

Personality

One of the most important skills that a successful SharePoint business analyst can have is good "people skills". In some form, you will probably be interacting with different people at an organization more than what a full-time developer or administrator would. There will be times where you will need to keep people calm during challenging periods, build rapport with people who might feel their job is being replaced with technology, build bridges between departments who don't want to work together and leave people feeling that the services you provide are worth what they paid for. Some of the most important personality traits I have found that worked for me over the past ten years in working with SharePoint are:

- Not blaming people when mistakes happen, just finding a solution to the problem
- Being extremely patient and understanding
- Never acting arrogant or superior because you may know more than someone else about SharePoint
- Being willing to compromise
- Going the extra mile to think things through up front and being very pro-active in delivering solutions so they will be a success when they are delivered to clients and stakeholders
- Creating and keeping clear and concise documentation
- Creating realistic and well thought out project and architectural solution plans
- Being able to appear confident even if you do not have an answer at the time, you can research it and get back to people later
- Knowing how to politely say "no"
- Be a champion of the project and treat stakeholders with a sense of urgency, overcome political issues that might arise and resistance from some people who don't want to use it or see your project succeed
- Lead by example, encourage and empower users

Certifications and Obtaining Experience

I have been asked a few times about how do get the job without the experience, and how do you get the experience without the job. This usually also brings up the discussion regarding SharePoint certifications and if they are worth getting. Being that I am a Microsoft Certified Trainer, I admit that my opinion is a bit biased toward trying to get at least a couple of them. However, the decision is always your own to make. Also, at this time, SharePoint certifications are in a bit of limbo. A certification doesn't guarantee that you are truly skilled in a job, but it does show that you were willing to take enough time to study and pay for it which can translate into commitment. Also, I can honestly say, having SharePoint certifications has gotten me a lot more job interviews than others because it is something that looks good on a resume.

Now to the "limbo" situation surrounding SharePoint certifications. At the time of writing this book there isn't really a current end user SharePoint certification available. There is still an end-user SharePoint 2013 exam (Microsoft Office Specialist 77-419) available to take and it is really the only end-user based exam out there at the moment. The other SharePoint certifications are much more specific to either being an administrator or a developer and require a series of exams. Additionally, if you are interested in discounted Official Microsoft Training or certifications at a bulk discount, I can assist you as I am currently a Microsoft Learning Partner and Microsoft Certified Trainer. Lastly, since this topic will continue to change as SharePoint evolves and Microsoft Learning changes, I have created an addendum page on my website to refer to for the most current information. Visit http://www.matthewjbailey.com/sharepoint-business-analyst/ to see the current options in this category.

Finally, before I wrap up this sub-topic, I wanted to list a few ways you can build your resume with relevant skills in case you are having a bit of a challenge trying to get your foot in the door. Here are a few suggestions:

- Try finding a non-profit to volunteer your services for in exchange for being able to use them as a reference on your resume
- Try going to user groups to network and meet others who might know of job openings
- Try taking a custom course (such as the one my company offers) that gives you an "unofficial SharePoint business analyst" certification
- Try getting a business analyst certification from IIBA
- Try finding an internship
- Try expanding your role at your current job to include some BA job duties

Most importantly, don't stop trying. Even for myself, things don't always happen on the first try and I have been turned down for job opportunities as well. Persistence and learning why what you are doing isn't working, then changing that will help you go farther down the road.

Continuous Learning & SharePoint Knowledge

You may have noticed that in the tech industry the pace of change has accelerated to a level faster than ever before. SharePoint is no exception to this rule. It falls into the category of a very mature technology (having started out as the Tahoe server around 2001ish) that is now trying to play catchup with modern, open-source technologies to stay relevant. It has gone through its periods of highs around 2011 and seen some decline due to people putting too much in it or doing too much with it where it could not support the user demands put upon it. There are now many versions of SharePoint available and they are split between on-premises, hybrid and Office 365 cloud versions. I will go into determining which version of SharePoint you have with which features in future chapters. It is important to realize though that at the moment, even if you learn SharePoint, there will be an on-going and continuous commitment on your part needed to keep up with all of the new features, changes and deprecations happening within the product. Make sure you have the level of interest and time available to make this commitment.

Finding Problems to Create Solutions

At some organizations part of your job might be creating and finding work to keep yourself and others on your team working. Finding inefficient processes and problems with business processes that can be improved via SharePoint are something you will want to become good at. First understanding what SharePoint is good for and not good for will help.

Here are some examples of what types of solutions others have created with SharePoint successfully:
- Company intranets
- Communications and information repositories for companies and employees
- Automating paper processes that are usually handled by multiple people or chains of approvals

Somethings that SharePoint is in debate to be used for:
- Public facing websites and extranets

Somethings that SharePoint is <u>not</u> good for:
- Very large repositories of files of decent size.
- Applications that will have many different users who all need very specific security at a very granular level on large amounts of data
- Too many complex workflows performing multiple actions repeatedly
- Applications that need constant, real-time searchable data to be surfaced

The Mindset of Creating and Delivering "Success"

To wrap up this chapter, I think it helps to understand that your end goal should always revolve around "success". This term is a bit vague I admit, but in general, you are probably going to want to be a part of:
- A project that is a success
- A SharePoint system that runs successfully (without too many errors, slowness or issues)
- A project that solves a business problem successfully
- A team that can deliver project on-time, in budget with SharePoint successfully

Each project is going to have its own definition of what success is. Some projects might require you to meet all of the above specifications and the specific project business and functional requirements. The later part of the last sentence, in my opinion, is what is most important. If there is not a very specific agreement of what you are building, how you are building it, how it will be delivered and maintained then it will be far, far too easy to declare something that was built in SharePoint was not a success. We will need something, that our stakeholders (customer) can make a clear, specific explanation and agreement to so we can deliver "success". The majority of this book will focus on this topic, getting everyone on the same page and having the same understanding of what is being delivered so you, too, can be a "success".

Let's start building the foundation of our road to "success"…

THE SHAREPOINT BUSINESS ANALYST GUIDE

2. PREPARING TO MEET WITH STAKEHOLDERS

Everyone's SharePoint projects will be different. You may already be at a job where you know the people you work with. Others might be thrown into a new consulting gig where the client expects you to create miracles starting day one. In either case, preparing for anything that might happen as you join the project is essential. This chapter (as much of this book does) will offer a great deal of information, however you most likely will need it all. Thus, read through it but know you will most likely only pull parts of it as needed when you finally meet with your stakeholders.

Software Used by SharePoint Business Analysts

Before you meet with your stakeholders it is good to know which software programs will aide you in your work. I have listed several that I have used myself as well as others people have mentioned to me throughout my speaking engagements. Some analysts prepare a PowerPoint presentation, some have mockups, some have a questionnaire, some use all of it. To help you decide what will work best for your situation and organization, I have provided some detail on the pros, cons and purpose of each. Of course you won't need all of these but you can decide which ones based on cost, organizational governance and availability will work best for you. As a note, I have not been compensated in any way to promote any of the items listed below.

Product: Questionnaire specific to SharePoint for requirements	**Have I Used It?** YES!!!!
Purpose: A very detailed of questions to ask stakeholders prior to beginning a project authored by yours truly.	
Pros: This is my personal questionnaire (included in my book) for your personal use. It is the cumulation of 10 years of lessons learned to help you avoid many of the SharePoint pitfalls that occur for others.	
Cons: The document is long and detailed. Thus, review it once in detail, then just take out the parts that you need for your particular project.	

Product: SnagIt	**Have I Used It?** Yes
Purpose: A screen capture and short video capture tool.	
Pros: SnagIt also allows you to mark-up photos with notations and bullet points to turn images into informative visual documentation. A unique feature is that is allows for "rolling" screen captures (meaning if you trying to capture an entire web page you would have to scroll down several times to see, the tool automatically scrolls down and captures the entire page in one image).	
Cons: Small cost ($49 at time of this writing).	

It is not quite as feature rich as something such as Adobe Photoshop.

Product: Camtasia	**Have I Used It?** Yes
Purpose: Video recording and creating tool	
Pros: Great for creating pre-recorded webinars/meetings. Great for creating video training materials.	
Cons: It can be a bit harder to learn due to it being more complex, however if you can spend a few hours learning it I think it is a great tool. The cost can be a bit high.	

Product: Microsoft OneNote	**Have I Used It?** Yes
Purpose: Documentation & Collaboration	
Pros: Comes will the Office suite so you will most likely have it accessible to you. Great for taking meeting notes and has a feature to add meetings to a OneNote page. Great for putting different types of media (video, documents, typed text, images) all one page.	
Cons: Not quite as fluid for documentation like Word.	

Product: Microsoft Word	**Have I Used It?** Yes
Purpose: Documentation & Collaboration	
Pros Comes will the Office suite so you will most likely have it accessible to you. Great for creating most of your requirements. Can be saved in multiple formats.	
Cons: Not as good for things that should be in Excel (like tables, etc.).	

Product: Axure	**Have I Used It?** No
Purpose: Wireframing & prototyping	
Pros Sketch& Wireframe Flow Diagrams Advanced Prototyping Mobile Prototyping Notes and Documentation Axure Share Publishing Used by many large organizations. Works with Agile and Waterfall methodologies.	
Cons: The product is not free, however cost seems minimal: $29 per user monthly or $495, also available for team and enterprise pricing (prices as of time of this writing).	

Product: Balsamiq	**Have I Used It?** Yes
Purpose: Wireframing & mockups	
Pros: Low cost, very popular.	
Cons: I personally found this tool hard to use. I am not sure if it is can create "interactivity" in the mockups (demonstrating moving steps). The graphic choices for visual representation is not attractive out of the box.	

Product: InVision	**Have I Used It?** No
Purpose: Design prototyping	
Pros: FREE!!!! Get high-fidelity in under 5 minutes. Upload your design files and add animations, gestures, and transitions to transform your static screens into clickable, interactive prototypes.	
Cons: Unsure if this is more tailored for apps vs. multi-device SharePoint site visual prototyping.	

Product: Visual Studio Team Services	**Have I Used It?** Yes
Purpose: Storyboarding Agile Tools Git integration Continuous Integration Package Management Release Management Centralized version control system with free private repos. Cloud based load testing -tools for manual, performance and automated testing.	
Pros: Most parts are free for up to 5 users. Part of the Microsoft family of products (and actually built partially on SharePoint on the backend). Very feature rich for a free tool.	
Cons: Only works with Agile, Scrum or CII methodologies. Can take a good amount of time to setup a project with all of the stakeholders involved. Free version limited to 5 users, additional users are available for purchase.	

Product: mindjet	**Have I Used It?** Yes
Purpose: Mind mapping	

Pros: Made for "brainstorming."

Could help define roles and business processes.

Could aide in bringing out sub-conscious thoughts users have they might be afraid to say.

Appears to offer more structure templates to avoid the random, endless thought problems that can occur.

Can add files from SharePoint (possibly via Zapier).

Cons: Sometimes the number of thoughts and ideas can grow so large and out of control that it becomes unusable.

It can generate a lot of ideas that excite users that you may not be able to implement because of how SharePoint works or the restrictions at the organization you are at.

Other software used by SharePoint Business Analysts:
- UXPin
- Adobe Comp CC
- Relative Wave Forms
- JUSTINMIND
- Microsoft Planner, Flow, Groups & Teams (Office 365)
- Microsoft Project
- Visio
- PowerPoint's Storyboarding tab
- Adobe Story
- Excel
- XMind

Preparing to Meet With Stakeholders

When preparing to meet with stakeholders, is important to know who will be attending which meetings and what their purposes are. Many times you exposure to certain stakeholders is limited and making sure you can politely get down to the exact details needed from the meeting is imperative. When I plan for a meeting, I personally do the following:

- Figure out who will be attending, what their job role is and their possible interest in the project
- Figure out what stage of the project we are in (i.e., total beginning, half way through a bad project, phase 2, etc.)
- Understand what it is people are expecting to accomplish in this meeting (i.e., demonstrate what SharePoint can do, discuss time consuming issues they are having with manual processes that could be automated, create a new project, etc.)
- Find out the agenda of the meeting, assess how long you have to meet and attempt to set certain amounts of time for each topic that will be discussed

I usually try to ask my direct manager to find out the answers to these questions. If they are not available, I then may try to email a main stakeholder I will be meeting with for answers. You may not find out everything, however knowing this information upfront will allow you to prepare

-

Who is a Stakeholder?

"Anyone who can cause an issue, receive a benefit from or affect your project." – Me

Do We Have the Right Stakeholders Involved?

One major issue I see in SharePoint projects is not fully including all stakeholders. Remember, at least for myself, a stakeholder is anyone who could affect your project. This could be the change management team, the IT Windows Server administrators, budget managers and budgets, people "talking negatively" about your project and even the CEO of the organization should there suddenly be a mass layoff that would cancel your project. Now I understand you might not be able to get a hold of all of these stakeholders, but you should absolutely get a hold of as many of them as you can and make them aware of your project, their role, and politely ask for their planned solution. Here are just a few examples of stakeholders that might not be normally thought of:

- IT / Administrators (Windows, AD, InfoSec, SQL, SharePoint, etc.) / Infrastructure / Architecture / Developers / Help Desk or Support
- End users / Other developers/project teams (not directly on this project)
- Past parties involved with project (if needed)
- Change Management
- Managers (related or ones whose actions could put a stop to everything)
- Project Managers
- Trainer / end user adoption

* What is each person going to get from this project? I ask this question to get stakeholders involved of their own volition, not by forcing or begging them to be involved.

Real-World Example of Improper Stakeholder Assessments

I was on a migration project once where there was an entirely separate Windows Server and security team. We were moving an entire SharePoint farm from one data center to another. Parts of our site were an extranet that required SSL certificates. Due to the company's finances, they chose to create their own certificates from Windows Server. Now the issue – the person creating the certificates was not involved originally as a stakeholder. After the project started, we realized the person in charge of this had not done it for a very long time and had quite a few issues. This cost us a week of lost time as many other parts of the server configurations and testing were dependent upon this item being completed.

Example Stakeholder Assessment Document

Below is an example of my stakeholder assessment document. It is included at the end of the book in the *Sample SharePoint Requirement Templates* section.

Stakeholder Assessment Document							
Stakeholder Name	Stakeholder's Contact Information	How much impact does this person have on the project?	How much influence does this stakeholder have over the project?	What is this stakeholder getting from this project?	What role & responsibilities will this stakeholder have?	What could this stakeholder do to cause an issue with your project?	What is your plan on keeping this stakeholder engaged?
Henrietta HumanResourceManager	hhr@fakecompany.com	High - She should be considered project sponsor	High	A new image to project to the company about the HR department. A new, more modern way to communicate with other HR employees.	Approving the design. Approving the site structure and site functionality.	Change their mind far too often, need signoff on approvals.	Send weekly updates and demos to show progress. Ask for feedback occasionally to see how she feels the project is going.
Cathy Communicator	cc@fakecompany.com	Medium - co-author of site	Low - Henrietta didn't seem to think Cathy's opinion mattered much unfortunately.	A way to communicate to the organization items happening in her division of human resources.	Authoring content in one section of the site.	Complain a lot possibly. Not complete her section of the site content.	Send updates only when something affects her portion of the site. Have a training meeting on how to use the site to encourage her to complete the rest on her own.
Andy ITAdmin	aa@fakecompany.com	High - if he does not deploy site we are at a stand still	Low - Henrietta has too much clout a roadblock.	Standard job responsibilities.	Deploying the site to production.	Not deploy the site.	Give Andy updates on project dates to make sure he will be available on deployment day.
Patty ProjectManager	ppm@fakecompany.com	Medium - in charge of budgeting, timelines and persons related to project.	Medium - Patty could bring up issues that could move their way up the pipeline of employees or mark the project on her status reports as not going well.	Credit for the project being deployed successfully.	Budgeting, timelines and persons related to project.	Mark the project on her status reports as not going well.	Daily updates on where we are at with the project plan, any potential issues being discovered. stakeholders not being as engaged as they should be, etc.
*The persons listed in this document in blue are examples, please delete them before using this document in production.							

Example of a stakeholder assessment document. This template is included in this book.

Environment, Environment, Environment!

In real estate, it's "location, location, location". In SharePoint, for myself, it's all about the environment as your first step. If you don't know your environment, you will create mass frustration for yourself, lose valuable time, risk projects failing, make commitments you cannot keep along with many other things.

Can you answer the following questions about your SharePoint environment?

- What version are you on?
- Are you fully on-premises, in the cloud or a hybrid mix? If hybrid or on-premises, how or is there a mix?
- Are certain features turned on or off?
- For on-premises, do you have the standard or enterprise edition and complimentary servers?
- Has there been restrictions placed on what you are allowed to do by a governance team (i.e., no full-trust code, no client-side scripting, no add-ins, no site collection admin access, not allowed to certain web parts, etc.)
- How is your search configured?
- Do you have user profiles or Delve or the Office Graph?
- Are you allowed to use Azure?
- Are you allowed to use Flow, PowerApps or other Office 365 products?

Below you will find the checklist I ask either an IT manager of the SharePoint administrator to understand what type of environment I am working with. You will also find this is in *SharePoint "Conversation Starter" Requirements Questionnaire* at the end of this book.

* As some companies have hybrid or comingled environments, you may end up selecting more than one option in this section.

Edition (s)

	Office 365 Development Tenant
	Office 365 Business
	Office 365 Business Essentials
	Office 365 Business Premium
	Office 365 ProPlus
	Office 365 Enterprise E1
	Office 365 Enterprise E3
	Office 365 Enterprise E5
	Office 365 Enterprise K1
	Office 365 U.S. Government Community G1
	Office 365 U.S. Government Community G3
	Office 365 U.S. Government Community G5
	SharePoint Online managed tenant (*like Office 365 but Microsoft manages it and does not update like Office 365 does*)
	SharePoint 2016 Standard & Office Web Apps Servers
	SharePoint 2016 Standard & Office Web Apps Servers
	SharePoint 2016 Enterprise
	SharePoint 2016 Enterprise
	SharePoint 2013 Foundation
	SharePoint 2013 Standard
	SharePoint 2013 Enterprise
	SharePoint 2010 Foundation
	SharePoint 2010 Standard
	SharePoint 2010 Enterprise
	SharePoint 2007 Enterprise
	SharePoint 2007 Standard
	WSS 3.0
	SharePoint 2003
	Other version _____

Configuration

	100% on premises
	100% Cloud (not VMs in cloud, Office 365 cloud)
	Hybrid (*explain*)

Service Applications Enabled

	Application Management Service
	SharePoint Translation Services
	Access Services 2010
	Access Services
	Business Data Connectivity service
	Excel Services Application
	Managed Metadata service
	PerformancePoint Service Application
	Search service
	Secure Store Service
	State service
	Usage and Health Data Collection service
	User Profile service
	Visio Graphics Service
	Word Automation Services
	Other _____
	Other _____
	Other _____
	Other _____
	Other _____
	Other _____

Development / Administration Tools Allowed

	Visual Studio
	Visual Studio Code
	SharePoint Designer
	InfoPath Designer
	PowerApps
	Flow
	PowerShell ISE
	Other _____
	Other _____
	Other _____

Development Methods Allowed

	Full Trust Solutions (on-premises servers only)
	Provider Hosted Add-In (app)
	SharePoint Hosted Add-in (app)
	Client Side Scripting
	Page Layout Customizations
	Master Page Changes Allowed
	Other _____
	Other _____

Third Party Server Based Addons / Software Purchased

	Nintex
	Metalogix
	ShareGate
	K2
	Other _____
	Other _____

Having a Development Environment and Test IDs

After you clearly understand what your current environment is, you will want your own development testing environment set up the same way. Many places may not have this available to you or won't give you access to what you need. These days, getting your own SharePoint environment of almost any type is just a few dollars and a few clicks away. Your options include an Office 365 develop account, an Azure server farm, a rented virtual CloudShare or your own test lab on your own computer using trial or free software.

Don't let someone else's "no" stop you from obtaining "success".

The "S" Word – Do I Mention SharePoint in the Beginning or Not?

Another question I receive often is "Do I even mention SharePoint?" -- It depends. Personally, when someone hires me it is specifically because they already have SharePoint and know they want to use it do something with, thus I don't have that issue occur too frequently. The reality is that there have been a lot of poor SharePoint implementations or poorly maintained SharePoint projects and not everyone has a high opinion of the product. However, if you are in a situation where you asked to come in to create a solution for a project and you are unsure about the user's response to the word "SharePoint", here is some advice on when you might or might not want to mention it.

Mention It:
- You and the stakeholders already know they will be using SharePoint regardless of their feelings toward it.
- When validating requirements and your concept for a solution.
- When you are scoping requirements and managing stakeholder expectations.

Don't Mention It (yet…)
- When you have not identified the business purpose yet.
- When you have not completed the "Environment, Environment, Environment!" section of this book so you know what you will be allowed to do with SharePoint.

Requirements? Who Has Time for Requirements?!

One of the most frequently asked questions I receive is "We don't have time for requirements, what do we do?." My stomach turns when I hear this, but it is reality. Many consulting companies or management disorganization create situations where they do not budget in time for any requirements. Personally, I will refuse any jobs where this is the situation because I have learned a very important lesson:

"The more rushed, unavailable and unwilling stakeholders are to talk through what the end result of the project should be – the higher the likelihood it will end up as a project failure."

That being said, I have included some ideas for you to use on how to convince stakeholders to take the time to create requirements *(this is regardless of which methodology you are using, the requirements may be created in different formats or timeframes, but the need to do them still applies)*. See some questions I ask or articles I use below:

- Would you have a custom house built without approving blueprints?
- Would you buy a stock without knowing what the company is all about or how it is performing?
- Would you pick a surgeon to perform neurosurgery without researching them?
- Have to figure out what's in it for them *(also referred to as wii.fm)*
- How will this benefit them, what are they getting from it
- Can this save them time or hassle, is there a negative consequence by not doing it (last resort)
- CIO analysis: Why 37 percent of projects fail: http://www.zdnet.com/article/cio-analysis-why-37-percent-of-projects-fail/

What is a Requirement?

A requirement is something wanted or needed that is within the constraints of the scope of the project and the systems abilities. Requirements are not undocumented notes, conversations or ideas that have not been agreed to in writing in your documentation or tracking system.

One lesson I have learned personally is that when a stakeholder ends up saying "I think", it usually won't end up being a very good requirement so be sure to follow up until you get an "I'm sure". True that the requirement may change, but at least the responsibility of the change has fallen off of your shoulders in this situation.

Requirement Types: Knowing When to Use Which Requirement Document

Business Requirements: Business requirements are high level requirements that management and a board of directors would typically understand. The emphasis is on what is required, rather than on how to achieve it.

- States the 'why' for a project. "The system will allow users to enter data on each customer call and notate the current status to track inbound calls."
- "Creating an employee asset deployment tracking system that allows configuration and support teams to document their work and management to monitor it."

Functional Requirements: Functional requirements are very detailed and outline exactly what needs to be delivered and would typically be read by business analysts, developers, project manager and testers.

- Outlines the 'what' for a project. For example, if the business requirement is to create an asset deployment system as listed above, the functional requirements may outline how each support team will interact with the system, who has access to the system, how the managers will view the data, who will have ownership of the data and which time, what type of SharePoint site (list or library) would be used, etc.

Technical Requirements: A technical requirement pertains to the technical aspects that your system must fulfill, such as performance-related issues, reliability issues, and availability issues and/or how the system will be built. Examples include:

- What is needed to support the project during implementation, development and ongoing delivery. Any emergency outages will be responded to in less than 2 hours.
- The system will ensure a 99.9% uptime with non-emergency planned outages being given one week notice.
- Managing server logs to see if workflows produce errors.
- Monitor the performance of the SQL Server database storage.
- Provide server and network response times of lower than ___ seconds to save a form over an average period of time.

Data Type Diagrams: Clearly defines the data types of each field   This field will be of type multi-line rich text field.

Flow Diagrams: When your project requirements become more complex (Visio)   Defines the process of how things will flow before you build a workflow.

Prototypes / Mockups / Wireframes and Screenshots: Hierarchical site structure mapping   State the structure of a site, assists with UI/UX.

Testing Requirements: Should always come back to verify the deliverables   Having a user perform a specific set of tasks to validate a specific requirement works as agreed upon.

Technical Specifications: Example of a proposed architecture, how a system would be built or architected. Example on how I would build an app and the restrictions in place that might prevent this so that I might obtain approval to deploy it.

Use Cases or User Stories: Examples might be something like step-by-step instructions, 1. Go to website 2. Click on login 3. Enter username and password 4. You are redirected to the start page.

Technical Specifications: Example of a proposed architecture, how a system would be built or architected.   Example on how I would build an app and the restrictions in place that might prevent this so that I might obtain approval to deploy it.

Transition Document: Assist with implementation or delivery.   Steps related to staff training and knowledge transfer to users once the project is completed.

Mind Maps / Maps & Collaboration Games: A mind map or concept map is a visual representation of hierarchical info   A mind map is a graphical way to represent ideas and concepts. It is a visual thinking tool that helps structuring information, helping you to better analyze, comprehend, synthesize, recall and generate new ideas. Just as in every great idea, its power lies in its simplicity.

- Promotes critical and subliminal thinking.

Stakeholder Analysis: To gauge which stakeholders you should invest the most time and effort in. Used to evaluate the importance, roles, responsibilities and possible issues each stakeholder could cause or what they could contribute.

Methodologies

There are a number of methodologies out there used for larger IT / SharePoint projects. However, I have really only come across a few in 10 years of working with the product, thus I will review them here. It is also important to note, that at many organizations there was is **no** methodology even being used. In my opinion, for smaller projects, it isn't necessarily mandatory to have a methodology in place. However, for complex or large and time consuming projects, it is important that all stakeholders involved have some methodology or plan of action in place. Which one will work for your organization is going to be up to the amount of time your business stakeholders will make available to you, the skill level of the developers and administrators and if there is already a mandate in place at your organization on what they are using. Let's briefly discuss a few of these now.

Waterfall

The waterfall model is a linear sequential (non-iterative) design approach for software development, in which progress flows in one direction downwards (like a waterfall) through the phases of conception, initiation, analysis, design, construction, testing, deployment and maintenance.

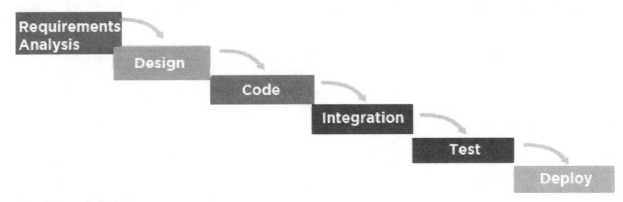

Example of Waterfall phases.

Disadvantages of Waterfall

- This model is simple and easy to understand and use.
- It is easy to manage due to the rigidity of the model – each phase has specific deliverables and a review process.
- In this model phases are processed and completed one at a time. Phases do not overlap.
- Waterfall model works well for smaller projects where requirements are very well understood.

Disadvantages of Waterfall Model

- Once an application is in the testing stage, it is very difficult to go back and change something that was not well-thought out in the concept stage.
- No working software is produced until late during the life cycle.
- High amounts of risk and uncertainty.
- Not a good model for complex and object-oriented projects.
- Poor model for long and ongoing projects.

Agile

"Agile" has definitely become a bit of a catch-phrase as it has grown in popularity the past few years. The problem with this is that many teams say "Oh yes, were agile", but don't really understand the concepts of it or follow the methodology fully. Alternatively, when you have many smaller, frequent request for change, agile can increase implementation times tremendously.

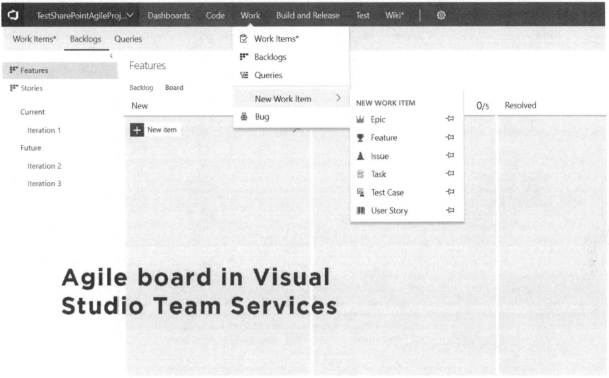

Example of the Agile setup in Visual Studio Team Services.

The Agile Project Management Framework takes a different approach to product/software development. Requirements in the form of capabilities are defined and prioritized. A backlog of these items is built and maintained on an ongoing basis. New capability is planned in a series of Iterations or Sprints which are short in duration. Each iteration goes thru a cycle to deliver the target capabilities. The combination of Iterations rapidly delivers more and more capability in the product or software over time.

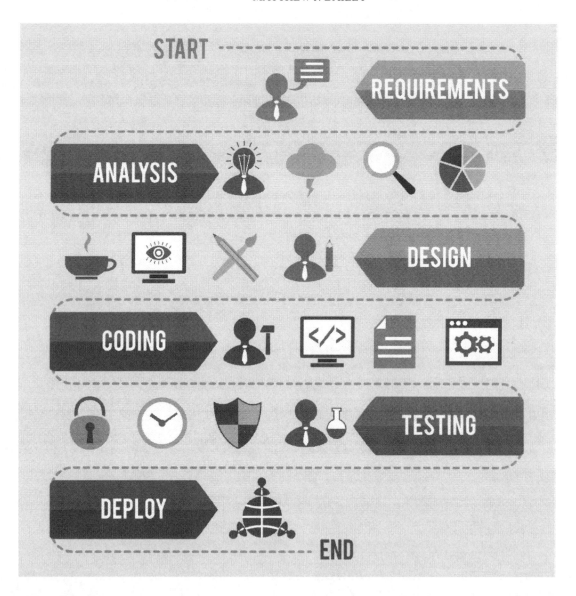

Elements of Agile
- The high-level processes that need to be supported by an Agile project for a SharePoint solution include
- Backlog Management
- Iteration (Sprint) Planning
- Defining the Active Agile Sprint Plan
- Iteration Management (e.g., Sprint tracking)
- Agile Sprint Status – the Sprint Tote Board
- Sprint Burn Down List

Advantages of Agile
- People and interaction are prioritized over process and tools
- Continuous attention to excellence and good design
- Early return on investment
- Build the right products
- Continually deliver better quality

Disadvantages of Agile
- Difficult to assess the effort required at the beginning of the software development life cycle, have

to estimate by sprints
- Potential for scope creep
- Very demanding on user's time
- Costs can increase as testers are required all the time instead of at the end
- Agile can be intense for the team
- Harder to implement in larger organizations who are used to working with Waterfall as others are used to working a different way with less involvement

Scrum – A Version of Agile

Scrum is an implementation of Agile. In my opinion, Scrum can demand a great deal of time from your stakeholders. Although it definitely has a "keep everything on track all the time" mentality which is good, I have rarely seen the business stakeholders making themselves available enough to make this work with SharePoint. This will have to be a decision you make by inquiring with your business stakeholders and your development team regarding if they will be able to keep these commitments.

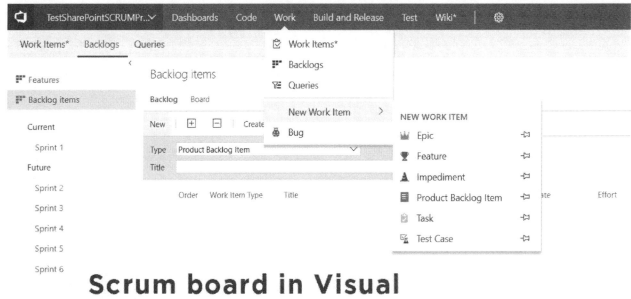

Scrum board in Visual Studio Team Services

Scrum example menu in Visual Studio Team Services

Kanban – A Tool Used in Agile

Again, scratching the surface, Kanban is also a tool used to organize work for the sake of efficiency. Like Scrum, Kanban encourages work to be broken down into manageable chunks and uses a Kanban Board (very similar to the Scrum Board) to visualize that work as it progresses through the work flow. Where Scrum limits the amount of time allowed to accomplish a particular amount of work (by means of sprints), Kanban limits the amount of work allowed in any one condition (only so many tasks can be ongoing, only so many can be on the to-do list.)

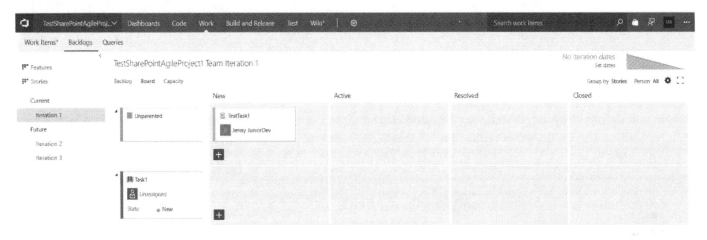

Image from Visual Studio Team Services of an Agile Kanban board.

Conclusion

Agile is a very popular project management method. It is especially useful in managing rapid deployment of new product features in measured cycles. SharePoint 2013 can be leveraged as a platform for managing Agile projects.

Agilefall

This is my personal favorite. It is basically taking the best parts of Agile and Waterfall and making your own methodology in sorts. I find that in the beginning of a project that the structure of Waterfall can help a lot to ensure that the stakeholders understand what the business process and project end-result (or success) looks like. However I find that the Agile concept for change requests is more efficient and faster to implement ongoing or last minute changes to the requirements.

Agile vs Waterfall Methodology

Traditional Project Management or Waterfall framework assumes a deliberate progressive set of activities that fall in order. There is a definite start and end to this approach and this method doesn't support rapid deployment easily. Here are a few bullet points about each methodology. My personal preference is for what I refer to as *Agilefall,* which is a combination of both methodologies but applied depending on the situation.

On a recent very large, custom SharePoint project I worked on, I had to decide when to use which methodology to complete the project. The project had many, many stakeholders involved and many of them were not sure of what their business process was. There was also difficulty in obtaining stakeholders time as needed along with very strict governance regulations in place at the organization.

Listed below are some of the tasks involved with the project and why I chose to use which methodology at that time.

The Requirements Gathering Phase: Waterfall

In the beginning of the project I found the stakeholders to be "running amuck" and lacking organization, clear thought and understanding of their thought process. I did not feel that starting a build immediately was a good idea and chose to go with several meetings creating and refining requirement regarding their business process (workflows), the security involved from each team and other factors before investing time in programming.

First Demo / Prototype: Mixed

After weeks of meeting with stakeholders and starting to build out a basic prototype of the system to demonstrate to stakeholders at an upcoming meeting. Small changes that I knew I could make in a few minutes perhaps could be referred to as agile, however there were larger requests that would take a lot of time and I chose to go back and alter the original requirements for more sign-off prior to investing prolonged amounts of time programming.

Business Process Changes: Mixed

As the flow from team to team and the workflows behind the scenes responsible for this changed, I had to stop and think about the stakeholder issue of changing the requirements so often that it was going to lead to project issues and prevent me from delivering "success". I intentionally started to slow the work down and require meetings with walkthroughs and sign offs as well as padded time frame estimates on the work. I hope this doesn't sound bad, but it is a reality that when stakeholders start to lose sight of what you are doing as the business analyst, administrator or developer, they need to be brought back down to reality. Constant, on-going changes made from desperation of a high pressure project can affect the deliverable of your SharePoint project tremendously. Try whatever you can to not get as caught up in other people's issues as it will drag your project down.

Additional Field Requests & Small JavaScript Changes: Agile

In this case, my ability to start using agile processes made a lot more sense. It was actually refreshing after weeks of challenging work to move into a phase where smaller, simple changes were being requested. It was easier to get a stakeholder on board to be a part of the implementation process and use some of the agile tools listed to track the changes.

Summary

Here is a quick summary of thel the reasoning I use to determine which methodology to use in my projects:

<u>Waterfall</u>

- Good for helping stakeholders figure out what their business process is
- Better if you know you are not going to get much of the stakeholders time
- Can be slower and requirements can change before completion if you follow the methodology in a very rigid manner
- Harder to convince stakeholders to take the time to invest in the process, depends on my ability to convince the stakeholders to get on board with this

<u>Agile</u>

- Needs a lot more time and commitment from stakeholders
- Harder to estimate the amount of time needed to complete an entire project
- Customer satisfaction regular adaptation to changing circumstances
- Feedback from real customers becomes part of the process and aides in implementing change quickly
- Good for lots of small, ongoing updates and changes that need to hit production quickly

3. MEETING WITH STAKEHOLDERS

Now that we have covered the preparation needed to meet with stakeholders so that we exude a knowledgeable, approachable attitude to them, let's review some items to keep in mind while you are actually meeting with your stakeholders.

When it comes to meeting with stakeholders, the biggest lessons I have learned has been the following:

1. Making the most of the time you get, as you most likely will never end up getting as much as you truly need
2. Managing their expectations. Most business stakeholders are not technical in nature and don't understand that they might be asking for unrealistic amounts of features or functionality to be built into a system.
3. Trying to help them figure out what they actually need and can be done within the allotted budget and timeframes.
4. Getting the stakeholders to understand their role and commit to the time and deliverables needed from them to make the project a success.
5. Clarifying and/or explaining the differences between SharePoint and everything else (i.e., "can you just make it like Facebook?" or "Can you make it like how my iPhone works?"....um, no.)

Keeping these in mind, let's move onto a few more things to consider during your meetings or workshops.

Agenda

Their agenda and your agenda vs. the time you have to meet. This is usually a challenge. As mentioned in the previous chapter, I try to send an agenda prior to meeting with stakeholders so we can ensure everyone's expectations are on the same page. In some cases, I actually break out time allotments to how long we will be discussing each item so we can cover everything needed. I play the "timing each topic" idea by ear however as some stakeholders are very casual and some stakeholders might be upper level management with limited time and I don't want to come across with a bad impressions to them.

Beginning , During and After Your Meetings

- Introductions & using the stakeholder assessment document included with this book (you might be able to get some of the information to fill this out prior to the meeting depending on if others or a project manager is able to fill you in on this information).
- Discover which stakeholders will have the final say on which parts of the project so you can plan for their sign-off prior to a full build.
- Agenda – preparing it and sticking to it
- Asking the right SharePoint questions and understanding what the stakeholder's definition of "success" will be (what their user objectives are) – Using my *SharePoint "Conversation Starter" Requirements Questionnaire* included with this book.

- Taking notes.
- Follow up items for each person, reiterate as you wrap up the meeting who has a task to do and when they could do it by (that might include yourself too).
- Send out meeting minutes afterwards to all attendees (or invited attendees that could not attend but are still going to be active in participating in the project).

Obtaining What You Need (Even if the Stakeholders Don't Know What It Is)

There have definitely been times where I have met with stakeholders and by asking certain questions, it has opened a door to the stakeholders not really knowing what it is they are needing. In cases such as this, there will usually be tasks assigned to them to figure this out and possibly having them contact others to obtain the answers. In addition to this, a few techniques I have seen some SharePoint analysts use to help users extract their thoughts and business processes are:

- Collaboration Games. These are games setup to collaborate with others on the team (your stakeholders) to find a way to come to agreement on what their needs are. This is a little different than just hashing out a discussion about the topic and is more interactive. (*Note: I am not an expert in this area, however I have listed an addendum to some great examples and others in the SharePoint community who have specialized in this area. Please see http://www.matthewjbailey.com/sharepoint-business-analyst/).*
- Asking questions in the *Site Purpose & Business Need* section of my *SharePoint "Conversation Starter" Requirements Questionnaire.*

Follow up after meetings

Personally, I always send out meeting recaps. I usually take the notes in a OneNote book and then share the link with all attendees. I also may assign tasks from the meeting in a SharePoint list and add all of these items to a home page of a SharePoint site to track the project. Whatever works for you is most important, but it will depend on what software you have to work with mostly. Many companies I are not willing to spend more money on high grade project management software.

4. SECURITY & COMPLIANCE IN SHAREPOINT (OFFICE 365)

*NOTE: This chapter might be overwhelming at first, however I wanted to go into all of the features, behaviors and options SharePoint and its correlating technologies offer to allow you to make the best security decisions for your SharePoint project.

Security...this chapter might be a bit challenging to understand if you have not worked with the security features of SharePoint / Office 365. I have often been asked "Is SharePoint secure?" or "How can I get stakeholders to sign off that the application I built in SharePoint is secure?". I wish there was an easy answer to these questions. However, the answer isn't quite that simple.

There are a lot of different security and compliance features available. Some of them overlap in features. Some of them might be used in conjunction with others. Some are meant only to monitor behavior vs. others that are meant to actually restrict access. With so many options, I will cover the available features with their strengths and compatibility. However, it is very possible you will need the SharePoint administrator's or InfoSec administrator's help to setup these features. If you happen to be in a role where you are both the SharePoint administrator and the business analyst, I would suggest going to the Microsoft website for detailed instructions on how to setup these features (although some might be a bit challenging to do so).

To help you understand the security-related features of SharePoint and Office 365 (SharePoint Online), I have organized this chapter into different sections that could affect SharePoint being secure:

- Built-In Features & Services in the SharePoint & Office 365 to Enable and Configure
- SharePoint site collection level (and below) configuration regarding security
- Human behavior, compliance and governance regarding security

If you would like to learn more about this check out my addendum page found at http://www.matthewjbailey.com/sharepoint-business-guide/

Built-In Features & Services Microsoft Gives You in the SharePoint & Office 365 to Enable and Configure

IRM
You can use Information Rights Management (IRM) to help control and protect files that are downloaded from lists or libraries. IRM adds another layer of security beyond simple permissions and prevents fine-grained actions like printing a document or forwarding an email. The service is available on-premises and in Office 365 (SharePoint Online.) It can control more than just SharePoint documents. However, the on-premises version is Active Directory RMS, and it is Azure RMS in Office 365.

IRM has to be configured at the tenant level and library level to function properly in SharePoint as seen in the images below.

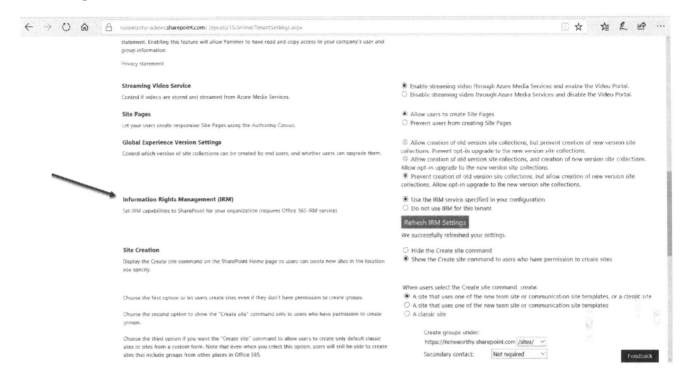

Example of enabling IRM at the tenant level in the SharePoint administration center in Office 365.

Service Engineering   ✏ EDIT LINKS

Settings › Information Rights Management Settings

Information Rights Management (IRM)

IRM helps protect sensitive files from being misused or distributed without permission once they have been downloaded from this library.

☑ Restrict permissions on this library on download

Create a permission policy title:

[   ]

Add a permission policy description:

[   ]

HIDE OPTIONS

Set additional IRM library settings

This section provides additional settings that control the library behavior.

☐ Do not allow users to upload documents that do not support IRM
☐ Stop restricting access to the library at

☐ Prevent opening documents in the browser for this Document Library

Configure document access rights

This section control the document access rights (for viewers) after the document is downloaded from the library; read only viewing right is the default. Granting the rights below is reducing the bar for accessing the content by unauthorized users.

☐ Allow viewers to print
☐ Allow viewers to run script and screen reader to function on downloaded documents
☐ Allow viewers to write on a copy of the downloaded document
☐ After download, document access rights will expire after these number of days (1-365)   30

Set group protection and credentials interval

Use the settings in this section to control the caching policy of the license the application that opens the document will use and to allow sharing the downloaded document with users that belong to a specified group

☐ Users must verify their credentials using this interval (days)   30

☑ Allow group protection. Default group:

[   ]

Example of creating an IRM policy at the library level in the library settings in SharePoint.

DLP

Use data loss prevention (DLP) policies to help identify and protect your organization's sensitive information. For example you can set up policies to help make sure information in email and docs isn't shared with the wrong people. DLP allows you to integrate its service with other products. As an example, if you were building your own custom add-in, you could integrate DLP with it.

Azure Rights Management

Using Azure, each file is encrypted and must be opened using a client that supports Azure Rights Management such as Microsoft Office. You must be connected to a network to be able to use this service because the client must contact Azure RM each time you attempt to open or modify the file. Azure RM was built mostly for SharePoint Online and the other Office 365 suite of products where you store supported files. However, you can use it with SharePoint Server on-premises with a connector that you install.

Auditing

After setting up auditing policies, it allows you to view who has edited or read documents within SharePoint. The Office 365 version also offers a rich search experience that includes items outside of

SharePoint as well. Auditing is not a tool to restrict access. It is a monitoring feature to create an audit trail for content and user activity.

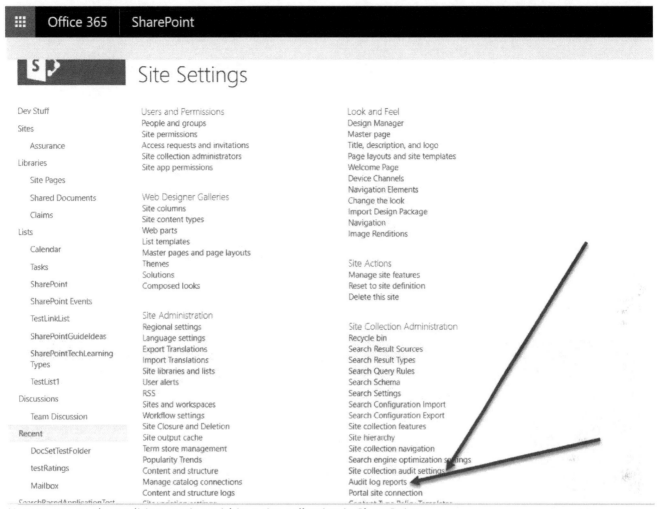

How to access the auditing section within a site collection in SharePoint.

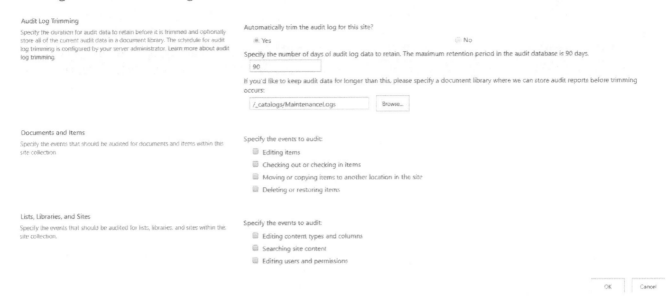

Configuring the audit settings at the site collection level in SharePoint.

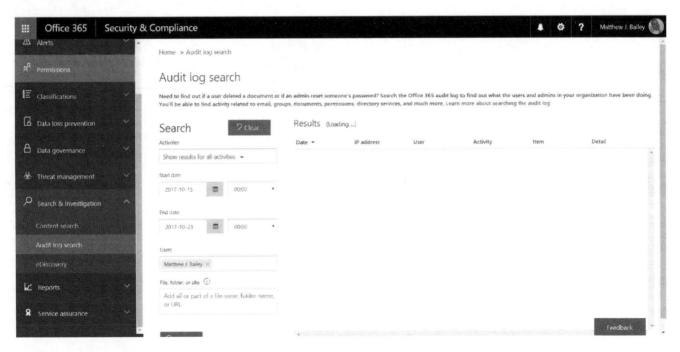

Example of the auditing center in the Security & Compliance center in Office 365 where you can search for the events you set up in the auditing settings at the site collection level in the screenshots above.

Two-Factor Authentication

From the title, this is pretty self-explanatory. It basically means your users will have to authenticate twice to access content. This is a once per session activity. If the user goes to look at many different documents, they will only be prompted once to perform the double authentication in the very beginning. Microsoft has an app to download titled *Microsoft Authenticator app* and is available for download for iOS and Android. After logging in with two-factor authentication, you will receive a prompt from this app to compete the second step of authentication.

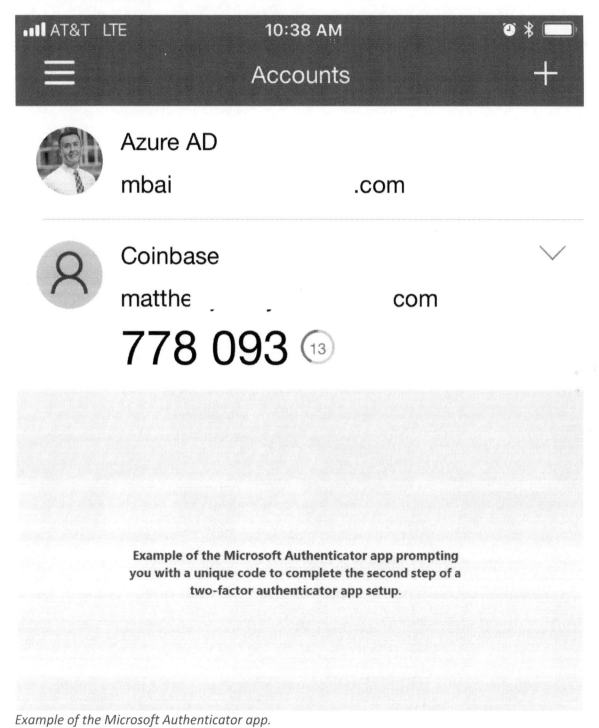

Example of the Microsoft Authenticator app prompting you with a unique code to complete the second step of a two-factor authenticator app setup.

Example of the Microsoft Authenticator app.

MDM

Another option for Office 365 (and possibly InTune) is Mobile Device Management. MDM policies are applied to groups of users (it will affect all of the user's devices) and they can enforce Conditional Access to Exchange Online, SharePoint Online and OneDrive for Business through any of the supported mobile applications.

With Conditional Access, when a user logs into Office 365 through a supported mobile app, the app checks with Azure Active Directory to see if the user is subject to a Conditional Access policy. If the user has a policy assigned, and the device is not marked as enrolled and compliant, the application prompts the user to enroll the device in MDM. In the case of an Exchange ActiveSync (EAS) client, Exchange sends an email with a link to enroll. Once the user has enrolled the device, the device settings policies are sent to the device, and the user must update the device to meet the appropriate settings such as PIN and encryption. After the settings are updated, the agent on the device informs the management service, which in-turn marks the user's device as enrolled and compliant in Azure Active Directory.

Restrict access based on device or network location

These settings apply to content in SharePoint, OneDrive, and Office 365 groups.

Get Enterprise Mobility + Security

Create conditional access policies to protect your organization's information

Learn more

Unmanaged devices

Control access from devices that aren't compliant or joined to a domain. The setting you select here will apply to all users in your organization. To customize conditional access policies, save your selection and go to the Azure AD admin center .

To use this setting, get a subscription to Enterprise Mobility + Security and assign a license to yourself. Manage subscriptions

Apps that don't use modern authentication

This setting applies to third-party apps and Office 2010 and earlier.

- ⦿ Allow
- ○ Block

Control access based on network location

☑ Only allow access from specific IP address locations
Allowed IP addresses

Use commas to separate IP addresses and address ranges. For example: 172.160.0.0, 192.168.1.0/16, 2001:4798:80e8:8::290. Make sure you include your current IP address and that IP addresses don't overlap.

HTML Field Security

This is a simple feature that basically allows or disallows users to embed iFrames on SharePoint pages. It can be controlled at the site collection level in the *Site Settings.*

Human Behavior, Compliance and Governance Regarding Security

Compliance: HIPPA, GDPR

GDPR

If you do not live in Europe and do not do any business with anyone in Europe, you get a free pass to skip this section! If you fall into either category, unfortunately, you will have to work this into your project considerations.

In May 2018, a European privacy law, the General Data Protection Regulation (GDPR), is due to take effect. The GDPR imposes new rules on companies, government agencies, non-profits, and other organizations that offer goods and services to people in the European Union (EU), or that collect and analyze data tied to EU residents. The GDPR applies no matter where you are located.

Much like HIPPA, there isn't an "exact" answer on how to make things HIPPA-compliant. It is more about doing as much as you can to comply with the somewhat vague standards that comprise the GDPR. On a brighter note, there is a planned dashboard coming to Office 365 that will give you a GDPR score. Hopefully, this will arrive on schedule to assist everyone who must deal with the regulations.

There are also links to more information about GDPR on the addendum page of my website listed above.

HIPPA

According to the *Compliancy Group,* SharePoint Online is HIPPA compliant. I have included more links regarding this on my addendum page on my website.

Assigning and Architecting Permissions at the Site Collection, Site, List/Library & Item Level

First it is important to understand, from the site collection level and below, what SharePoint already has to offer. You can restrict or control access at:

- The top site collection level
- The sub-site(s) below (within) the site collection
- The library or list itself
- Each document or item within a list or library

Next you need to decide how to group your stakeholders and users of the SharePoint site to assign security. This will depend on if you are going to use:

- Active Directory groups (which may or may not already be created or be able to be created by your Windows Administrator)
- Create SharePoint groups within the site
- Use Groups in Office 365 (Which some people are referring to as o365 Groups)
- Assign users individually a permission

Pros and Cons of Using Which Type of Permissions Assignment

Active Directory Groups

Active Directory groups are usually controlled by your Windows Server administrator. Although there are ways to allow someone other than an administrator to create groups in Active Directory, they tend to be rarely implemented in my experience. The biggest drawback of AD groups is that you are dependent upon the Windows Server administrator to add or change the people in a group. This could create significant time delays regarding access and the ability to perform work depending on your organization.

The good thing about Active Directory groups is that, in many cases, they are connected to a new employee onboarding process and will usually include new employees automatically. They are also good if your organization has already set up these AD groups in a structure such as a region or department that matches the same levels of permissions you need to use for your SharePoint site. They are also accessible beyond just one site collection as they are Active Directory domain-wide in availability.

SharePoint Groups

SharePoint groups are still just groups of people. However, they are restricted to the site collection where they were created. They also cannot be used as email groups. A major benefit of SharePoint groups is that they can be created and edited immediately by the site collection administrator eliminating the need for another party to complete their task so your users can do their work. The group's owner may also manage the people inside the group. SharePoint groups also offer a membership request feature where users can request to join the group and an automated approval email can be sent to the group's owner.

Individual Users Being Assigned Permissions

Augh…this is an unfortunate reality of untrained or uninterested users managing your site and could fall into the governance arena. Sometimes your site collection administrators or those with full control permissions will just approve requests to join a site without looking to make sure they have been placed in a proper group. Alternatively, they will go to the *People and Groups* section in the site settings and just add a person individually instead of putting them in a properly named group. This is a very poor practice as eventually your security section of the site could fill up with hundreds of people randomly all having different permissions and it can be very challenging to track.

Planning Properly to Assign Permissions & Permission Levels

As a part of security planning, there is a section in my *SharePoint "Conversation Starter" Requirements Questionnaire* document that asks for all of the different roles your site will need. For example, you may have a couple of managers, some editors and many authors. This would be a total of 3 roles which should equal 3 groups of whatever type you choose. You can then put the appropriate people in each group and assign a permission level to that group.

Out of the box, SharePoint comes with several different permission levels to assign users or groups of users too. These permission levels are often just fine for a user's needs. However, there will be times when the default options are not appropriate for your needs. One example I often come across is giving the permission level to users that will allow them to edit or add new documents and /or list items but **not** allow them to delete anything. In this situation, I will create a custom permission level and name it something such as *Contribute No Delete.*

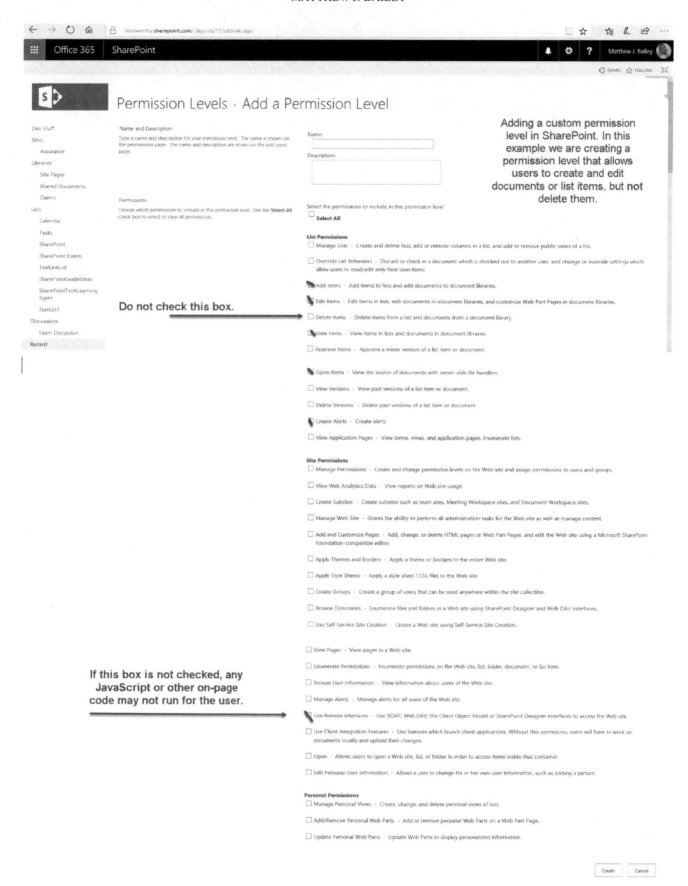

Example creating a custom permission at the site collection level.

SharePoint also allows for you to "break inheritance" and assign permissions separate from those that are assigned at the site collection level. If there is a library of documents that only certain people should be able to access, you can break inheritance and apply separate permissions to the library to secure it.

This same rule applies to specific list items or documents in a library. This is as fine-grained (without custom programming) as you can get with assigning permissions. If you want to try and secure parts of a document or only certain fields in a list item, you can only do this via programming. When assigning permissions at the list or document level, you should do so sparingly. I was on a project where the organization was using SharePoint Online (Office 365,) and I did not have control over the server resources. There were over 15,000 items with each list item having unique permissions. As more users started working on it at the same time, the site definitely ran into performance issues. This is just a word of caution to try and avoid such a scenario.

If Custom Development Has Been Performed.

When development has to occur in your project, there are additional security factors to consider. Since a human performs the programming, *how* the developer chooses to program SharePoint will determine if it is secure or not. Although very common, using JavaScript & CSS to hide items in SharePoint is not truly secure. You can easily do a right-click in the browser and select *View Source* to see the data. If you are using JavaScript to disable fields or grey them out, a user could turn off JavaScript in their browser *(unless your organization has disabled the ability for users to change their browser settings via an Active Directory Group Policy.)*

Full-Trust Solutions

The risk here is that developer could program almost anything they want. Think of this as the developer having the "keys to the kingdom". However, if you are in a on-premises environment and still using full-trust solutions, this is par for the course and there isn't much you can do about it. Just make sure you trust your developers and they aware of being careful when they program.

External Users & External Sharing

You can share a specific item in SharePoint via the *Share a Link* option At the moment, you need to have some type of Microsoft account (Outlook, Live.com or Office 365) to accept a sharing request as the external user. The person will appear in Azure AD after this, however it will not consume a license. At time of writing this book, Microsoft is scheduled to release a new feature that will allow external users to have documents shared with them without having a Microsoft account. Hopefully this will be implemented soon as I know many SharePoint users are looking forward to this feature. If the screenshots below do not look familiar to you, you are most likely using an older version of SharePoint and the screens might look a bit different with fewer options.

First, start your scope at the tenant level to decide if you want to allow sharing in the first place. If so, you can decide how you would like to configure it before moving to the site collection level. The admin center overrides all settings at the site and library/list levels.

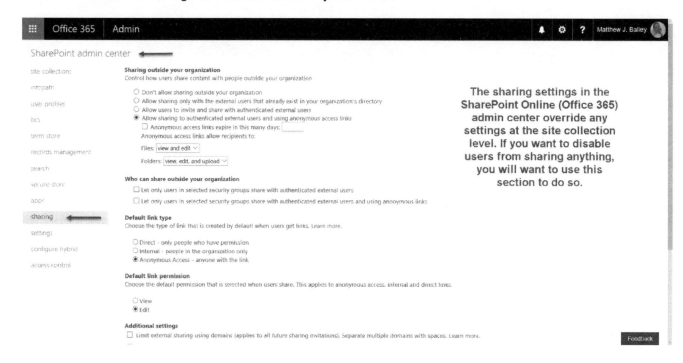

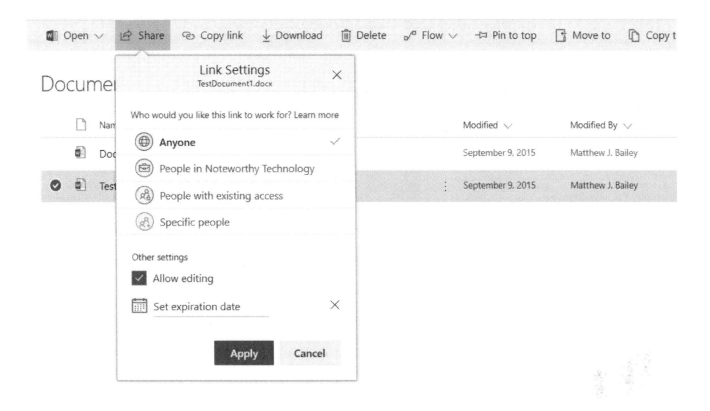

Example of the 'new' SharePoint document sharing experience (well, new at the time of writing this book at least).

Revoking Access for a Link That Has Already Been Shared With People

Sometimes a link has been shared with other users (internal and/or external) and you need to revoke access to it. When you create a sharing link, you have the option to set an expiration date, which is great. However, in urgent situations where you need to immediately revoke access from a shared link, I have included some screenshots below on how to perform this action.

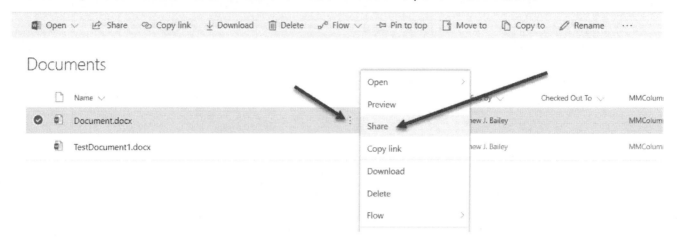

Step 1 in revoking access to a shared link to a document.

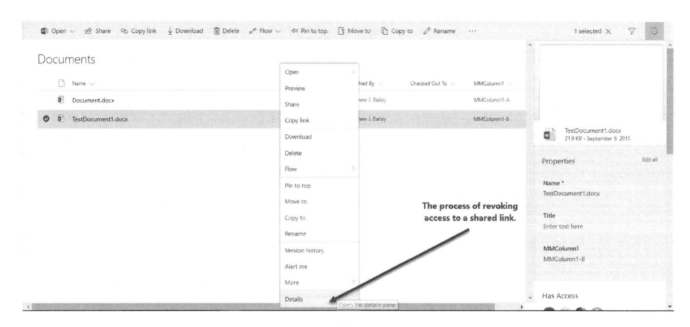

Step 2 in revoking access to a shared link to a document.

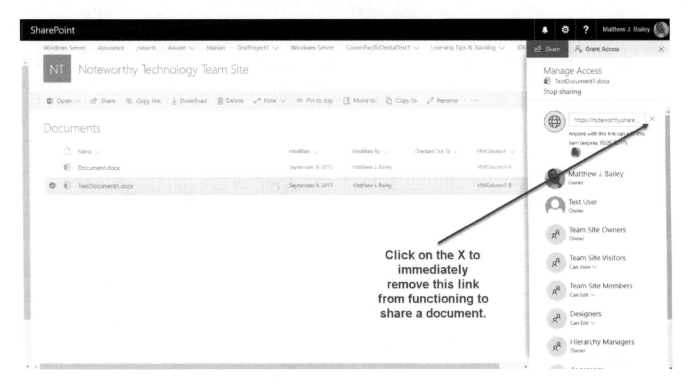

Step 3 in revoking access to a shared link to a document.

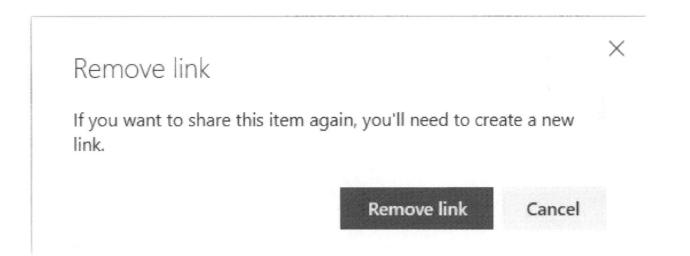

Step 4 in revoking access to a shared link to a document.

Other Human Errors That Can Create Security Issues

- Someone creating a script that needs a password and leaving the password unencrypted in the script or in a text file on the server. This was the cause of the Sony breach a few years back.
- Someone with full control or farm level administrator privileges who decides to "go rogue". Unfortunately, this is a human trust behavior and unless you have 2 people watching each other at all times or have disabled all email, screen shot, and USB drive abilities to share items there isn't much one can do about it.
- Someone with full control who decides to give others full control who haven't been formally trained. I have seen people giving access to people they shouldn't have, accidentally delete things, break things, you name it. Full control should be used sparingly. If possible when creating a new site collection for your users, you could create them as I saw at one of my clients where they were created from a custom template that has the ability to add other users with full control to the site access. This is one way to avoid this issue from occurring.

Summary

Wow, we sure covered a lot regarding security in SharePoint and its correlating technologies! As mentioned earlier, this can be very overwhelming. You may need to consult external or internal help with some of this. But remember, each area is a specific security concern which is a part of the entire concept of making SharePoint secure. There is no way to guarantee anything is truly 100% secure. You can only use as many of the tools and best practices available to make your SharePoint site as secure as possible.

5. CREATING YOUR SHAREPOINT REQUIREMENTS

The Right Requirement Documents For Your SharePoint Project

As mentioned in chapter 2, *Preparing to Meet With Stakeholders,* there are many different types of requirement documents available. It is now up to you to determine which documents are of importance to the project you are on. Also, if you are in a situation where you are only performing small change requests and ongoing maintenance, you may need few to none of these documents. It is up for you to decide. Ask yourself these questions:

- Are there a lot of different people involved?
- Is the project extremely detailed?
- Are you concerned about certain things such as adoption, governance, training, etc.?
- Are you getting a feeling of incomplete trust from some stakeholders where you want to put as much in writing as possible?
- Is there a specific business need this project is fulfilling or that was missing from a business process prior to you starting?

Stopping to think for a bit about which road the project is going to down should prompt you to grab the appropriate requirement documents listed above in this book (or possibly even some not included in this book).

If you have used my *SharePoint "Conversation Starter" Requirements Questionnaire* you will have asked many of the right questions so that you can create very detailed, specific requirement documents. If I haven't already mentioned it before, I almost always use images (usually placed in the addendums) in my requirement documents. Words can be misunderstood, but images with big red arrows, numbered sequences and text boxes explaining details of each column are hard to misunderstand. Admittedly, sometimes I refer to myself as Mr. SnagIt because I use it so often to take screen shots and add detailed notes to the images. Now, onto displaying some of my lovely artwork for you in some sample requirements documents.

1. Business Case Document

The business case brings together the benefits, disadvantages, costs, and risks of the reasoning or situation and future vision so that major stakeholders can decide if the project should move forward, be altered or not proceed at all. One might think that the items listed below or the reason someone is creating a SharePoint or Office 365 project would be worthwhile before they even ask for it. However, sadly, in my real life experience I have seen several instances of people asking for programs or features that really have little to no business value. Whether you choose to say anything about it will probably depend on your job position. If you work for a consulting company and you need to bill hours, you might not be as inclined to argue there is no business case for a project. However, if you are an internal employee with a vested interest in your organization, business cases might mean more to you.

What are some of the key ingredients in a well written business case document? Here are a few items:

- Business problem or opportunity
- Benefits
- Risks
- Costs vs. ROI
- Timeframes,
- Impact on operations
- Organizational capability to deliver the project outcomes

At the end of the book in the templates section, you will find a sample business case document to use.

2. Functional (User) Requirement Document

Functional requirements are very detailed and outline exactly what needs to be delivered and would typically be read by business analysts, developers, project manager and testers.
Outlines the 'what' for a project.

For example, if the business requirement is to create an asset deployment system as listed above, the functional requirements may outline how each support team will interact with the system, who has access to the system, how the managers will view the data, who will have ownership of the data and which time, what type of SharePoint site (list or library) would be used, etc.

This is the most important section regarding where my *SharePoint "Conversation Starter" Requirements Questionnaire (found at the end of this book)* comes into play. We are going to want to make sure we fully understand all of the following items before we start to create, clear and specific functional and non-functional requirements. You may also want to look at my sample *Functional Requirement Document* as this is where your specific requirements will be listed *(unless pursuing an agile methodology and keeping the requirements in a different format / location)*. As mentioned in my conversation starter document, we will want to review and be able to answer questions regarding all of the items listed here:

- SharePoint environment and setup
- Features enabled, service applications enabled and configuration
- Development tools allowed and development governance
- Third party products installed and available in your environment
- Identified the correct stakeholders
- Site purpose and business need
- User stories and/or use cases
- User roles in the site and security configuration
- User engagement (adoption) ideas
- Social interaction and collaboration
- Graphical design, UAT / UX ,visuals consistency
- Data submission, editing and viewing
- Forms and data capture
- Metadata and content types
- Web and content management
- Business process automation with workflows
- User management and functionality
- Accessibility and language
- Wireframing
- Build, test and launch plans
- Specific details of the deliverable
- Governance
- Items in and out of scope
- Risks & assumptions
- Timelines and budget

Using the template for this during your meetings and via follow up emails or conversations with stakeholders should allow you to obtain the answers you need. Remember, if you can't get the answers you need you may need to pause delivering the requirement and / or creating the statement of work. Being vague is one of the worst things, in my opinion, that you can do in the role of the SharePoint business analyst. It will almost always lead to misunderstandings, lost time and money, frustrations and lost trust and other negative occurrences.

Example Functional Requirements

Examples of functional requirements *(*REMEMBER – we want these be as detailed as possible to avoid confusion!!!)*

- Design: The site will follow the design demonstrated in Appendix A using the xxxxx theme to ensure it follows the same branding guidelines as the rest of the intranet.- Adoption Team
- Design: will be inherited from the existing theme named _____ that already is applied to the organization's intranet site. – Adoption Team
- Development: List based slider will be created and used on the homepage of the site. The slider will be controlled from a list that end users can change out the text, which items appear in the slider, allow the images in the slider to be clickable and go to specified URL, upload or change images for and create new slides for. The image within the slider must conform to the size of 1024 x 768. Example of deliverable is shown in Appendix 5.1 and Appendix 5.2. The list will allow for the following options:

  Field Name: Field Type
  1.   Title: Single line of text
  2.   Homepage Image: Hyperlink or Picture
  3.   Homepage Description: Multiple lines of text
  4.   Active: Yes/No
  5.   URL to link to: Hyperlink
  6.   The Title and Homepage Description are option text fields that would appear on the slider: Single Line Text
  7.   The active flag is used to determine if the image will appear on the slider. If checked the image should display: Checkbox Y/N
  8.   URL is an optional field that if populated, the image will link to that URL : Hyperlink

Example Non-Functional Requirements

Examples of non-functional requirements *(*REMEMBER – we want these be as detailed as possible to avoid confusion!!!)*

- File Types: All file types are allowed with the exception of the list outlined in Appendix 5.3 - SharePoint farm admin
- Search Availability: Files are available in search within 30 minutes however there are rare exceptions of up to a 24 hour wait. -N/A
- Onboarding process:New users will be added to the site along with the market based libraries (if on does not already exist) - Site Owner: This process / responsibility will be of the site owner.

Example Addendums displaying Detailed Visual Requirements

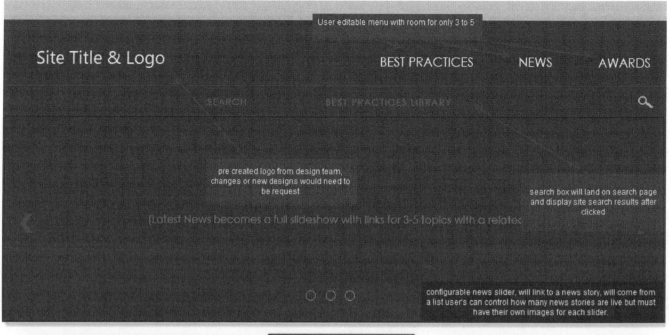
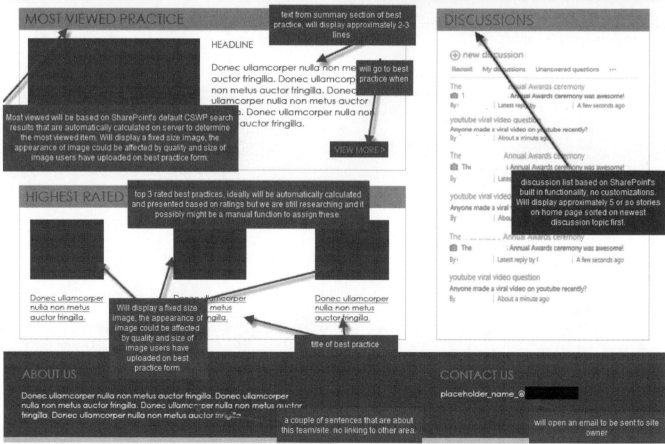

Example of a very detailed requirement addendum regarding how a home page will function in SharePoint. The organizations logos and wording has been intentionally removed to protect their identity.

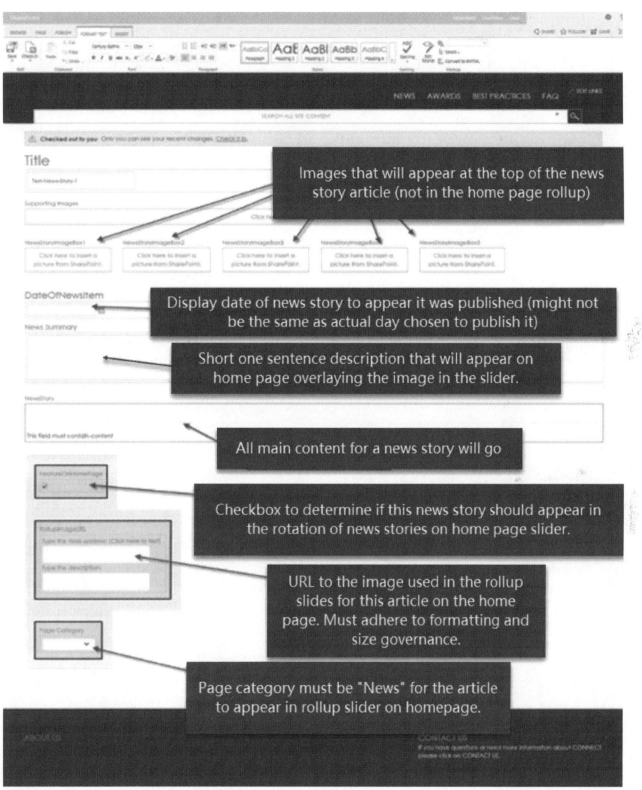

Example of a very detailed requirement addendum regarding how a news story page that will also include the ability to roll up to the home page in SharePoint. The organizations logos and wording has been intentionally removed to protect their identity.

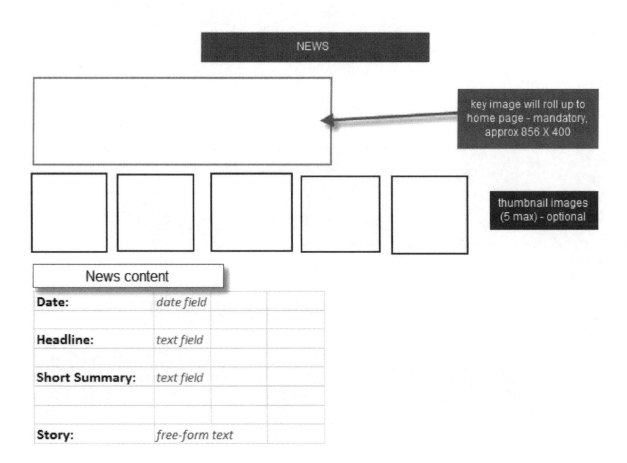

Example of a page mockup prior to building it in SharePoint.

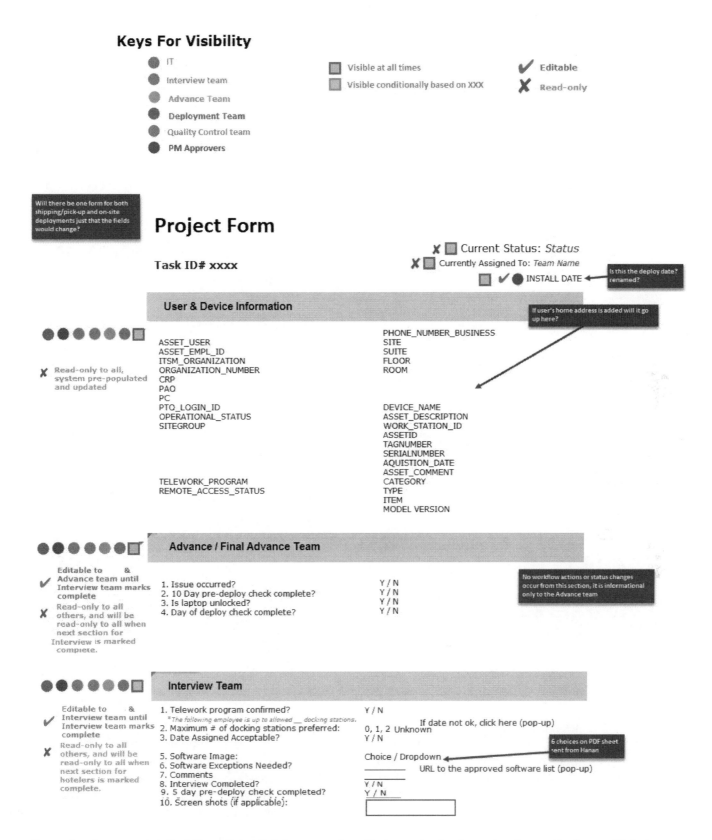

Keys For Visibility

- IT
- Interview team
- Advance Team
- Deployment Team
- Quality Control team
- PM Approvers

- Visible at all times
- Visible conditionally based on XXX

- ✔ Editable
- ✘ Read-only

Will there be one form for both shipping/pick-up and on-site deployments just that the fields would change?

Project Form

Task ID# xxxx

✘ ☐ Current Status: *Status*
✘ ☐ Currently Assigned To: *Team Name*
☐ ✔ ● INSTALL DATE ← *Is this the deploy date? renamed?*

User & Device Information

Is user's home address is added will it go up here?

✘ Read-only to all, system pre-populated and updated

ASSET_USER
ASSET_EMPL_ID
ITSM_ORGANIZATION
ORGANIZATION_NUMBER
CRP
PAO
PC
PTO_LOGIN_ID
OPERATIONAL_STATUS
SITEGROUP

TELEWORK_PROGRAM
REMOTE_ACCESS_STATUS

PHONE_NUMBER_BUSINESS
SITE
SUITE
FLOOR
ROOM

DEVICE_NAME
ASSET_DESCRIPTION
WORK_STATION_ID
ASSETID
TAGNUMBER
SERIALNUMBER
AQUISTION_DATE
ASSET_COMMENT
CATEGORY
TYPE
ITEM
MODEL VERSION

Advance / Final Advance Team

✔ Editable to & Advance team until Interview team marks complete
✘ Read-only to all others, and will be read-only to all when next section for Interview is marked complete.

1. Issue occurred?
2. 10 Day pre-deploy check complete?
3. Is laptop unlocked?
4. Day of deploy check complete?

Y / N
Y / N
Y / N
Y / N

No workflow actions or status changes occur from this section, it is informational only to the Advance team

Interview Team

✔ Editable to & Interview team until Interview team marks complete
✘ Read-only to all others, and will be read-only to all when next section for hotelers is marked complete.

1. Telework program confirmed?
   The following employee is up to allowed ___ docking stations.
2. Maximum # of docking stations preferred:
3. Date Assigned Acceptable?

5. Software Image:
6. Software Exceptions Needed?
7. Comments
8. Interview Completed?
9. 5 day pre-deploy check completed?
10. Screen shots (if applicable):

Y / N

0, 1, 2 Unknown
Y / N

Choice / Dropdown
_____ URL to the approved software list (pop-up)

Y / N
Y / N

If date not ok, click here (pop-up)

6 choices on PDF sheet sent from Hanan

Example of a very detailed SharePoint list form mockup that required column level security for multiple teams and varied during different statuses of the business process. Using color coded keys to create a form mockup such as this helped save a great deal of time by getting all of the stakeholders on the same page prior to spending so much time building out the form in SharePoint. The organizations logos and wording has been intentionally removed to protect their identity.

3. Other Requirement Documents

As described in Chapter 2, there are many different type of requirement documents you can use for a SharePoint project. I have also seen different companies merge some of the documents into just one document. However, there are a couple of documents I use often, I will list those below:

Field Data Type Document

I often use a *Field Data Type Document* or at least list the field data types within my functional requirements. I am seen many times where the stakeholders and the developers have a completely different vision of what that "column (field)" is supposed to be. Sometimes people forget to ask simple things like is this field a number, text, multi-line text, managed metadata, if it needs help text (description) or if it is required. This document help people think things through more thoroughly before you spend time building the application incorrectly.

A copy of this document can be found in the templates section at the end of this book.

Field Data Type Document

Form Name:	Billing Summary List Form			
Field Name	**Field Type**	**Field Description (user help)**	**More Detail**	**Required**
Title	Single line of text			Yes
Summary	Multiple lines of text		Enhanced rich text (Rich text with pictures, tables, and	Yes
Department	Choice (menu to choose from)			Yes
Department Code	Number (1, 1.0, 100)	Enter the billing code for the		Yes
Billing Amount	Currency ($, ¥, €)		Format should be British	Yes
Date of Bill	Date and Time	The date you want the bill to		Yes
Project Name	Lookup (information already on this site)		Looks up to project list	Yes
Needs Executive Signoff	Yes/No (check box)	Does this need a C level executive or above approval?		Yes
Billing Representative	Person or Group			No
Link to Project	Hyperlink or Picture	URL to the project site that was		Yes
Due Date	Calculated (based on other columns)		Add 30 days to Date of Bill field	Yes
Bill Sent	Task Outcome			Yes
External Content Type	External Data		Use the invoice content type	No
Project Tags	Managed Metadata		Use the managed metadata term set for project categories	No

Example of a field type document.

Technical Specification Document

I rarely use this type of document. I may include some of the technical specifications such as guaranteed up time, maintenance and other items needed to ensure that SharePoint is running almost all the time without issues in my functional requirements. However, I will list one exception where I did need to use a technical specification document. During a migration of an on-premises installation of SharePoint 2010 from one data center to a new host, I found this document valuable. I needed something to state that the new hosts data center was going to provide 24/7 support, the amount of resources such as CPU and memory per server, the number of servers and their roles (search, front end, etc.) and other technical items as a part of my project.

There are many other types of requirement documents (as listed in Chapter 2). Use what you feel will help you on the specific project you are working on and leave the rest for another time.

Usage Amounts, and Yes, Size Matters

Some of the biggest issues I have seen repeatedly occur with SharePoint that result in poor performance or errors popping up on the screen are due to:

- too many users
- too many items or documents
- very large of files sizes
- too many security scopes

It is important to ask your users questions relating to the items listed above or you could likely run into issues with longer term use and adoption. I have seen sites grow past the original amount of users, users adding too many items, users giving all the items unique permissions scopes and put large sized files in the attachments of list items. Since this was in an Office 365 / SharePoint Online environment where we had no control over the amount of server resources being allocated to our tenant, the prognosis was not good. We broke apart the system into different lists and sites to avoid some of the built-in SharePoint Online limitations, however I personally suggest you carefully consider the architecture when one or more of the items listed above applies to your project.

ROI = Build vs. Buy

There are going to be times when you will need to decide if after gathering all of the requirements, and knowing an estimated time and budget for a project, you will have to decide if purchasing a 3rd party product will be a better solution for your stakeholders than building it from scratch. This is where ROI comes into play.

Return on investment, or ROI, is the ratio of a profit or loss made in a fiscal year expressed in terms of an investment and shown as a percentage of increase or decrease in the value of the investment during the fiscal year and possibly future fiscal years. The basic formula for ROI is:

*ROI = Saved Amount from Project Returns / Total Investment * 100.*

Since SharePoint is about automating business processes and collaboration, I have used the term Saved Amount from Project Returns instead of the word "profit". If SharePoint had been created as an e-Commerce software, perhaps profit would apply. However, in almost all cases SharePoint is about reducing costs (via time, man hours, frustrations, improved organization, mismanaged or lost artifacts, etc.)

Other notes regarding ROI to take into consideration when determining the cost are:

- Licensing
- Maintenance
- On-going fees separate from the initial license
- Cost retraining new employees on the project should change requests occur with turnover
- Training
- Support hours costs

If ROI starts to look like it is going to kill your project and you don't want that to happen, a few tips I have are:

- Shorten the project into smaller phases so the total investment amount is shrank and focus on key features that will make large impact
- Add "low hanging fruit" to the project, meaning utilizing many of SharePoint's built in features to

add value and boost the project's appeal with the resources and budget you have to work with
- Try to cut out features that will only affect a small set of users or save only small amount of time or that are the "brilliant idea" of one of your stakeholders that no one else seems to think are quite so brilliant…but do so politely of course.

3rd Party Applications and Questionnaire

After fully evaluating your requirements and adding costs to them, you may find that exploring a 3rd party application to solve your needs is a better decision the performing custom programming yourself. Of course, there are pros and cons to this approach. I have specifically created a questionnaire titled *OFFICE 365 & SHAREPOINT "INTRANET IN A BOX": BEFORE YOU BUY IT* which is included at the end of this book.

The questionnaire goes into depth about purchasing a 3rd party solution for your SharePoint or Office 365 environment and the questions you should ask the vendor before you purchase it. Although this questionnaire was originally built for 3rd party "overlays" or "intranets in a box", I have found that I would use it for almost any 3rd party application review prior to purchase. Some of the items it covers are:

Why Are You Buying the Product?

- What is your purpose for buying this?
- Are you hoping to cut down on development times and costs?
- Are you hoping to supplement part of your development with this product for more basic requests from your users?
- Are you hoping to create a unified experience across your intranet?
- Would it be easier to let someone else deal with the constant changes that occur in SharePoint & Office 365?
-

Whatever your reason is fine, but make sure the cost of doing it yourself is not a better return on ROI than a purchase. Also, make sure the product you are purchasing (or renting) will meet the business needs you have.

Costs & Licensing

- Cost, per site, per person, annual fees, both, ask for real examples of total usage costs
- Uses – all intranet, hybrid with your own, hybrid with company adding more
- How does the pricing work for the product?
- Is it per user, per farm, per site, or possibly a combination of these?
- Is there an annual maintenance fee?
- Is there a separate cost to "launch" the product as a project at your company?
- Will there be additional costs from spending your own time training users on how to use the product or does the company provide training in some manner on how to use it?

Company & the Product

- How long has the product been in existence and how many versions does it have? If a vendor can say a few years and a few versions, this could be a good sign they are in it for the long haul and have ironed out some bugs.
- How much documentation and literature does the company have on the product? Also, very little documentation could be a sign that the company hasn't spent much time on this product yet.
- Does the company also offer consulting services? Do research on the company itself to see if the company has a good reputation.

SharePoint Specific Questions

- Are there any features, web parts or other things in SharePoint this product won't work with?
- Does the product work with foreign languages (variations / language translations)?
- Will the design apply to different search templates?
- Will simple things such as adding or changing a column on create issues?
- Is the web browser compatibility the same as what SharePoint supports?
- Did the company build their own custom web parts to use instead of the OOTB SharePoint web parts? How do they work, can you test them (see section on insisting on a live demo below)?
- Does the product support managed metadata navigation or have a mega-menu? How is it updated, are there limits to it?

- Are there any issues with different authentication scenarios such as federation, claims or single-sign on that would prevent certain assets of their product loading?
- Are the design files hosted within the SharePoint site assets, style library, a separate site collection or off-site such as CDN network on AWS or Azure?

Product Support
- If Microsoft comes out with a change that affects their software, what is the turnaround time to come up with an alternate solution or fix?
- What qualifies as a bug, free change and/or fix and what doesn't?
- Is the vendor following the strict branding guidelines on the Microsoft website?
- Will they allow you to customize the site vs. what they give you and will the support change? Are you even allowed to or able to change any of the code?

Please find the full copy of the document at the end of this book to use in your own real-world situations.

Wrapping Up the Requirements Phase

Did Your Requirements Answer These Questions?
- What is the business problem and how/what are we building with SharePoint to solve it?
- Scope (in and out of)
- Timeframes
- Stakeholders
- Warranties & Risks
- What and how data is capture, displayed and made available
- Security
- Who & how will it be managed and maintained
- Usage (frequency, amount of date, number of items, tracking)

Reality Check
Is it possible to complete this within the time and budget you have been given?

Meeting With Stakeholders for Requirements Review
Myself, I always meet with the stakeholders to review the requirements before providing a final statement of work and architectural plan. This will give the stakeholders to re-assess any requirements that might have changed or cut back (or even add) items that might be affected by the budget. Although you won't have an exact budget amount at this point, you should start to be able to get a feel regarding if it is way over or under the amounts originally discussed. I also like to meet with the stakeholders regarding the requirements to ensure what is planning to be built is completely accurate. This way I know when I gather the estimated project hours needed from the developers, project managers, administrators and the business analyst (and anyone else) I will have correct numbers to prepare the statement of work.

We are now ready to move onto the architectural planning phase to gather estimates, create a build plan and provide a statement of work (SOW) to our business stakeholders.

6. ARCHITECTING & PLANNING BEFORE BUILD

After finalizing your requirements, making sure that the ROI formula equates to the project being of value and getting some types of approval, it is time to plan out how you will build the project. There are two main objectives from this chapter to focus on:

1. Designing the project in the best way to accommodate the organization's needs (i.e. if security is the top priority, designing it most securely, or if cost is the most important factor, then building it as quickly as possible should be the top priority, etc.)
2. Obtaining estimates of work from all other stakeholders (especially the administrators, project managers if there is one and developers) so that you can provide an accurate statement of work (SOW).

When to Use What When Designing SharePoint Solutions

Quick Summary About Utilizing Some of SharePoint's Features
- Planning your site with a flat or segmented structure (site collection vs. sub-sites)
- Lists vs. Libraries – which to use when
- Folders – the bad, the ugly and the last resort
- Managed Metadata – pros and cons
- Workflows – SharePoint Designer, Flow or Workflow Manager?
- Classic or Modern experience

SharePoint: Structure & Hierarchy

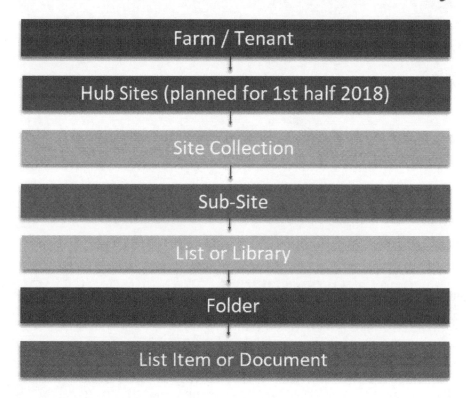

Structure of sites and artifacts in SharePoint, listed hierarchically.

Planning your site with a flat or segmented structure

First, you will need to determine how the structure of your site will be created. By this I mean, will you be creating separate site collections to segregate your content or will you be using one site collection with many sub-sites to segregate your content. At the moment, Microsoft has been advising people to use a "flat" architecture which means creating different site collections instead of one site collection with many sub-sites. The downside to this approach is that you will have issues with rolling up content from the different site collections to one area in the main site collection. There will also be issues with cross-site scripting if it is needed. As of the time of this writing, there is a planned new feature for SharePoint due sometime in the first half of 2018 called Hub Sites. This a new concept that will allow you to designate one site collection as the main parent for a group of other site collections. In a way this is just a different concept of creating the main site collection with many sub-sites. The power behind this idea however is that since many restrictions are placed at the site collection level, there should be less issues with Hub Sites and their related entities than trying to create many sub-sites inside of one site collection.

Libraries vs. Lists

Often you will come across the decision of whether to use a list or a library to store your artifacts. Sometimes it is easy to know which is best, but other times it might not be the easiest thing to determine. To assist your decision, I have listed the reasons you might select one over the other:

Lists:

- When you want a simple, top to bottom designed form, that easily can have new fields added or removed.

- Do not have a check in and check out feature like publishing pages do
- Can have attachments, but not recommended if you have many attachments per list item
- Some people say "the list is your data, but a library stores your data"

Libraries:

- When you want the design or layout of the page the user sees and enters data into to be something other than the default top to bottom structure list forms have.
- When you are storing purely documents (.pdf, Word, Excel, PowerPoint, etc.)
- When you need the publishing features enabled and an approval flow for each page to be published
- When you need versioning enabled (keeping copies of previous versions before the current version has been altered for reference or backup)

Not to confuse you, but technically "behind the scenes" a library is still a list. However, unless you start coding around them this isn't anything to worry about.

The "F" Word – Folders, Usually Not Your Friend in SharePoint

Folders in SharePoint have built up a bad reputation over the years. The preferred approach is tagging things with managed metadata terms instead. This way you can sort on the terms to create your views and organize your artifacts into groups instead of putting them into a folder. This being said, there are still rare exceptions when you may need to use folders and a lot of reasons regarding why you shouldn't use them. I have listed both of these below:

Why Not to Use Folders

- Folders don't display the number of items inside of them, if you have a lot of folders it is hard to know how many things are in which folder or if the folder might even be empty (think of it as a file share on a computer or server, just aimlessly opening folders trying to find something.)
- When you are in a particular sub-folder, there is no way to tell in which folder you are at any given time, and no easy way to navigate to the parent folder
- If you have assigned your artifacts a term from the term store (metadata), renaming words is easy. However it is hard to change folder structures.
- In classic mode sites, you only have one view to work with inside a folder. From my testing, however, it appeared you are able to create multiple views inside folders in Modern sites.
- When end users are in a hurry, they may not place documents in the proper folder. This happens more frequently than one might think.
- Security in folders is a bit different in its behavior.
- There is a URL length is limited to around 260 characters, if you create too many sub-folders you will run into issues.

Rare Exceptions When to Use Folders

I did have one exception where I needed to use folders. A site had over 5,000 items and over 5,000 unique permission scopes. I could have broken them into different lists or sites, but because of how the site had been pre-set up, I needed to be able to create views and searches that only searched from one list. Thus, I had to put list items into folders based on their status. Each folder had the permission instead of each item. This lowered the number of security scopes from over 5,000 down to 7 (seven).

Architecting (Mocking Up) Your Solution Build

When possible, I often try to create a quick mockup in SharePoint of the proposed solution. In other cases, I may have another demo I have already built in one my environments from a past project I can "scrub" and show to a business stakeholder or to work with the developer or administrator. Once again, I personally feel the value of visuals and interactivity brings understanding between all stakeholders to the highest level possible. You by no means will create an entire project as a demo for a client, but something that can display the key features to a user or business stakeholder so they understand how they will be performing their work in SharePoint adds immense value in my opinion. It also may start to get users excited about the project which is a key point in the adoption process.

SharePoint's Constant Change (Future Proofing)

One of the greatest challenges you will have with SharePoint, especially SharePoint Online / Office 365 is the constant change of features in the product. Watching the roadmap and subscribing to the weekly emails of changes for Office 365 are of the utmost importance. I have seen environments where changes, that could have been controlled in the administration center, rolled out to entire organizations of over 16,000 people. This resulted in confusion, many help desk calls and other issues due to "surprise updates". A governance plan for monitoring the constant change that comes from Microsoft is mandatory.

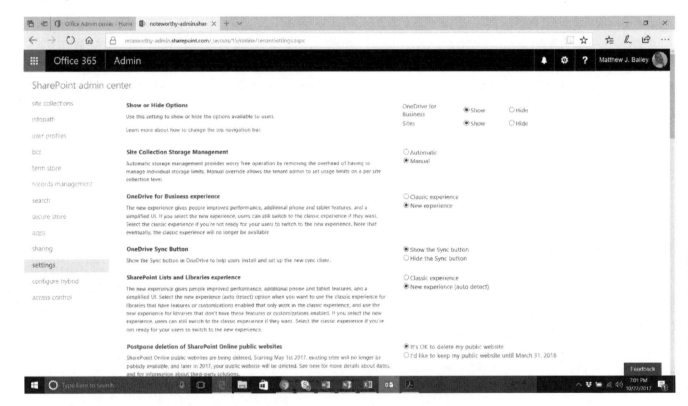

Example of the Office 365 Administration Center and the SharePoint admin center where the option to select the classic site experience should have been selected until the new modern sites that Microsoft pushed out to all tenants had been tested for compatibility within the organization.

Adoption: It Needs to Start Before You Build It

First, I should say that I am not what one would refer to as an expert in user adoption. However, I have been on enough projects to know that if you don't have the following items in place, the odds of your SharePoint project becoming an abandoned ghost town, the "angry talk" around the water cooler or the reason to blame you for something are very high. Since the user experience (UX/UI) are a part of what users will use to decide whether or not they system is usable or they like it, Adoption needs to be thought of before you begin the project, not after it has already become a problem. Some important things to consider as a part of any adoption plan are:

- The user interface and the ability to intuitively figure out how to use the system

- The speed and efficiency (few clicks as possible) of the system
- Having a "champion" stakeholder that will use the system to encourage or mandate that others use the system to and becomes "adopted" in your organization
- An ongoing plan to monitor and collect feedback about the system as time goes by
- Easy to find instructions, documentation or help notations throughout the system for users to figure out how to use the system (especially newer users who come to it later with no training)
- How the system will be rolled out (soft launch first to eliminate bugs, then actual launch)
- Training, user adoption and communication plans or workshops
- How support will be made available to users so that if issues occur they are not left feeling helpless

All this being said, Microsoft and some wonderful people in the SharePoint community will have more to contribute regarding adoption then I can offer in this short chapter. Please visit my blog at http://www.matthewjbailey.com/sharepoint-business-analyst/ and find the addendum on user adoption to find many more resources and people to assist with this topic.

Discussions With the Administrator (Even If It's You)
I am grateful to have played multiple roles in SharePoint projects including one as an administrator of a SharePoint farm. If the administrator is someone other than yourself, things to keep in mind that an administrator is thinking:

- It is the administrator's job to ensure the server is kept up and running and secure. Thus, the administrator at times might seem a bit "controlling", however it is understandable in some cases. Introducing new software, features or deployments to a SharePoitn environment can introduce problems, especially when the developers and stakeholders have not properly tested in an equivalent test environment.
- The administrator may want to prevent issues that start to creep up by users "overusing" InfoPath and SharePoint Designer, and it is possible they have turned these features off due to the problems they can introduce when pushed to their limits.
- Sometimes the administrator may be working in conjunction with other administrators (especially for on-premises deployments) such as a SQL Server administrator, information security and other administrators. Understand you may be communicating with more than one person in some cases to get your projects out.
- Some administrators must abide by governance or are personally "risk adverse" to cloud offerings such as SharePoint Online, Delve, Office Graph, Azure, Flow, PowerApps and more. This is argumentative. I see the point of where Microsoft hires external contractors and their own employees to monitor their servers that your data is stored on. This worries some people. On the other hand, Microsoft has spent over 1 billion dollars on cloud security features, which I believe is more than any other technology company. From an external threat (not including people with access already) perspective, it will be extremely difficult for your organization to compete or keep up with the amount of money and time Microsoft has invested in keeping your data secure.
- My advice for working with administrators is to try and understand their point of view and if you need to present ideas to them that they are adverse to, make sure you explain the business benefits and show the ROI as well as give them credit as a part of the project for the work being done. No administrator really wants more work, with potential issues and no credit for doing it all. Remember they are human too and you most likely get much further with your relationship with the SharePoint or Office 365 administrator.

Discussions With the Developer (Even If It's You)
Yes, I have worked as a SharePoint developer too! If the developer is someone other than yourself (or if it is you then feel free to just talk to yourself, hey I do it! – A bit more of my dry sense of humor,

grin…), some things I have learned from the developer's perspective are:

- A developer usually wants to try and learn new things.
- A developer doesn't like to be board or work on uninteresting features and projects.
- A developer usually doesn't think like an end user when it comes to the user experience *(of course there are exceptions to this rule).*
- Some (not all) developers, especially those who are working for an outside consulting agency on a fixed budget, will not always follow best practices, document their code or adhere to high standards.

This being said, the feelings and methods of how the developers will affect your project in different ways. Here are a few examples of decisions the developer could make that would affect your project:

- The developer may want to work with the newest technologies because they find them interesting. However, SharePoint is in a constantly evolving state. New features and correlating products like Flow, Azure Functions and the SharePoint Framework are the way of the future. However, some of these items are so new that they may not fully be able to replace the older technologies that are similar to them (i.e., SharePoint Designer Workflows, Timer Jobs and the add-in model). Also, with the SharePoint Framework, you can use different open-source programing languages such as TypeScript, Angular and React. This matters because of ongoing maintenance or future changes and the ability to find experienced staff to work with what has been built already. There isn't necessarily a completely right or completely wrong answer to how the developer chooses to build your project because SharePoint is in a state of flux, but be aware that their decisions matter and will impact you. *Note: I will say, that unless you are absolutely mandated to do so, try to avoid InfoPath at all costs as it will be officially deprecated at some point in the future.
- The developer hasn't or doesn't have an exact replica of your production environment to work in which can create errors when deploying, which equates to lost time and money
- The developer might mention new features coming or that have recently arrived such as SharePoint communication sites, SharePoint Hub sites, SharePoint Framework extensions, SharePoint modern sites, etc. This is usually my personal guideline on using new or coming features for all software:
  - If it is new, I will only use it if it has been out for a few months already in a production environment
  - If it expected to come, I usually will **not** wait for more than a few weeks for a feature to be released. I have seen too many times where features were on the SharePoint roadmap to be released at a certain time and were never released or released later than expected. I will come up with an alternative plan to create the solution in these situations.

*Note: Remember, these are just my suggestions from real-world experiences, how you choose to work with the development and planning of your SharePoint project is up to you.

Getting Your Estimates From Stakeholders

Your end goal in this chapter is to be able to create a final project plan, have approved requirements and the ability to create a statement of work for your business stakeholders or project sponsors to sign off on. Meeting with your developers and administrators I have found is the most important portion of this process. Here are some important tips for the discussions with these people so that you can obtain realistic estimates to create a statement of work (SOW).

- When a developer or administrator gives you an estimate, ask if they have performed this task before. I have found on more than one occasion that someone found an idea on the internet bu had not actually done the task in real life before. The solution didn't work and caused a lot of time delays trying to figure out another work around

- Ask if any of their tasks are dependent on other things or people. There could be delays out of control of the developer due to this. This could range from getting software needed to program in setup on their computer to needing someone's approval to do something from another department.
- Most administrators and developers will know to do this already, however make sure you "pad" their hours. It isn't meant to be dishonest, it is due to the nature of how IT works and the unexpected issues and changes that can occur during a project that you will have to accommodate yet be given no additional funding or time to complete. You will want that cushion of extra hours to fall back on when this happens. Of course, if you are on a fixed budget project that was undercut to get your foot in the door, you probably won't be so lucky in completing this item.

Providing a Statement of Work (SOW)

A statement of work (SOW) is a document routinely employed in the field of project management. It defines project-specific activities, deliverables and timelines for a vendor providing services to the client. The SOW typically also includes detailed requirements and pricing, with standard regulatory and governance terms and conditions. It is often an important accompaniment to a master service agreement or request for proposal (RFP). – *Wikipedia*

I have included a sample statement of work (SOW) template at the end of this book for you to use on your projects.

7. BUILDING YOUR SHAREPOINT PROJECT

During Your SharePoint Project Build

Depending on the methodology used on your project, having regular updates with your IT stakeholders and any deliverables due from your business stakeholders will vary. Whether you choose to have a daily scrum meeting, a weekly conference call or something else is up to depending on everyone's availability. The most important factor is to have these meetings and ask for visual representation and / or verification that each stakeholder is working on or completed their tasks with time estimates or that they will meet their given deadlines.

Timelines & How Will the Project Be Managed

Hopefully you should know by now which project management tool you will be using. The important piece, regardless of which tool you are using, is to make sure that the timelines that are set are realistic in the first place. Then, to keep close watch on them as each week passes. Keeping your business stakeholders and project sponsors up to date on any potential risks that start to creep up is also important, although you might want to be careful about how much you share so that it does not reflect poorly upon you.

Warning Signs To Watch For

Yes, it is a reality that SharePoint projects can run into a lot of issues, especially if the staff you have to work with is not intimately familiar with how SharePoint works and the skills needed to administer or develop within it. Here are some possible warning signs that things might start to be going sideways and some ideas on how to prevent them from turning into an unpleasant situation:

1. Important stakeholders start to consistently miss meetings
   o Sending emails regarding status of their attendance displayed in visual color bars has worked for me in the past (i.e. a big red warning displaying their number of missed meetings has exceed a normal threshold.)
2. Developers are not showing completed work
   o This is usually a sign of issues occurring on the development side. The problem is that it can difficult to determine if it is due to a lack of skill from the developer or due to the random, expected issues that will pop-up in every development project. Since I have done development before, I will usually start to ask things that more specific about the issue about why a deliverable hasn't been met. If a developer isn't able to go into rather specific details regarding why they are encountering an issue, this could be a warning sign regarding the skill level of the developer involved.
3. Random, consistent errors start appearing as you are working on the project
   o I usually find this happening when too many things are being implemented too quickly without proper testing. Sometimes it is better to see the errors during the development phase rather than having them pop-up in production anyways. The more you can test in a real-world scenario before production launch the better it will be for you and your reputation of being able to deliver.

Managing Scope Creep

- Create a process for requesting changes that will usually require manager approval to get the message across that change requests shouldn't be coming "willy nilly"
- My personal favorite response "Can we save this for Phase 2?"
- Know when to say "no."If you can't say "no then here are some alternatives:
    - Zero sum game. If something new goes into the scope, make sure that something comes out.
    - Start a back-log (or second project) for requests denied in the current project. Make this a prioritized list of features.
    - Price the scope creep. How much will you charge for added features? This might discourage some of the incoming requests.

Project Management Dashboard

If you aren't fortunate enough to have a high priced project management software at your disposal, I find just creating a project portal in SharePoint will work great instead.

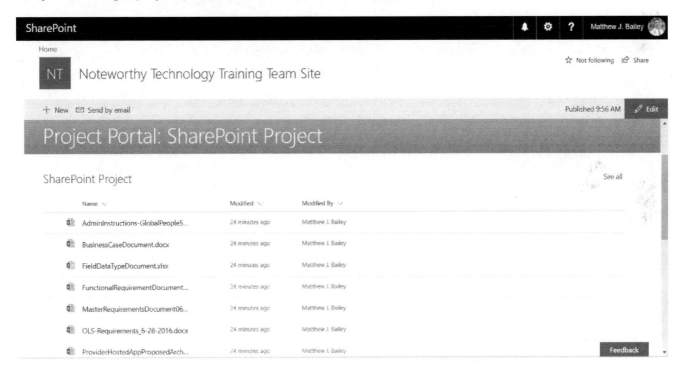

Example of storing project files and tasks in a SharePoint site to use as your project dashboard.

Consistent Updates to Stakeholders

Sending consistent updates with what you accomplished this week and plan to do next to important stakeholders.

8. TESTING, ROLLOUT & SIGN OFF

It might not be up to you to decide which testing method or tool will be used, however you will most likely be a part of the UAT process and need to ensure the application has successfully passed UAT to get sign off on the project deliverable. Testing in SharePoint has long been a difficulty people have faced. Unfortunately, there is no simple answer to this issue. I have listed below all of my knowledge on the topic, however, if you are looking for a quick and simple answer to all of your testing solutions, there might not be one. Here is how I personally deal with testing in SharePoint:

Manual UAT Test Script
When manual UAT needs to be done, I refer to my own UAT document which is included in the back of this book. One reason I like it so much is that it is extremely clear, details the steps to be taken to perform each test, provides visual examples, corresponds to an existing functional requirement number and requires an approval for each test from the stakeholders involved in testing. Depending on how you have written your functional requirement documents, you may be able to copy text and screenshots from them to assist you in creating your UAT documents at a rapid pace.

Example of My Manual UAT Test Scripts
I wanted to quickly show you an example of a specific test execution to get an idea about what I have described above.

4.1.4 Test Execution

4.1.4.1 Uploading Files
Validates Functional Requirement 1.2.1.1 (example)

*Note: Uploading is not built for responsive design so a laptop or computer must be used for this portion.

1. The home page should load with a slider functioning.
2. Click the *Upload Content* link, this should bring you to another page where you can select a market. This should bring you to a page with a *Files* tab at the top, now select *Upload Document.*

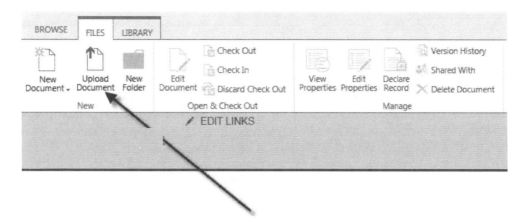

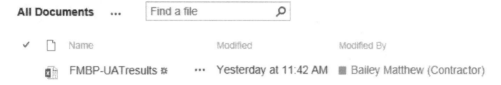

3. Now select the file you want to upload.

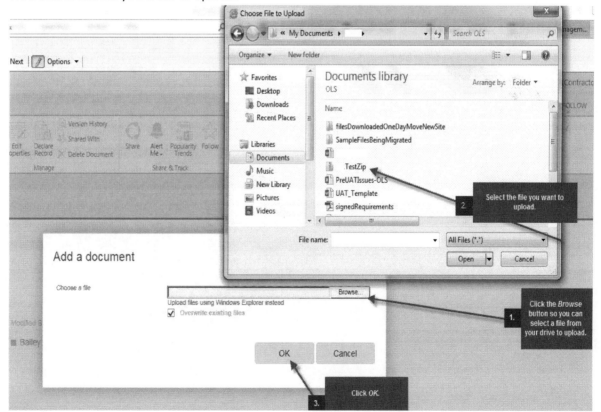

Fill in the form with data pertaining to the file that you have just uploaded.

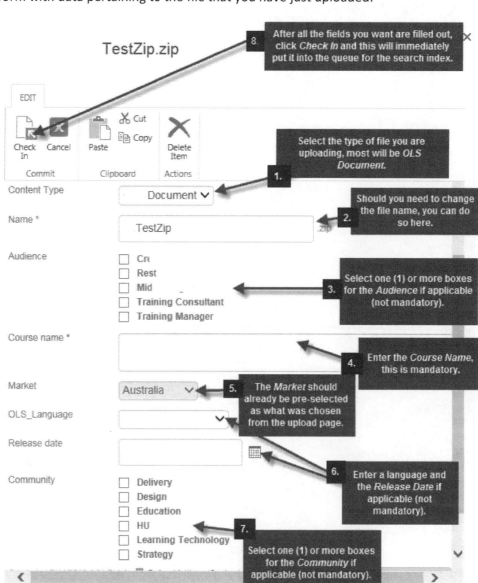

4. Verify the file is uploaded and checked in.

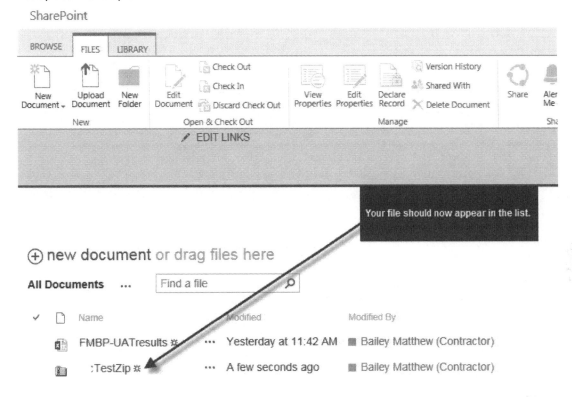

Test Result 1

Did this test pass or fail?

___PASS   ___ FAIL

Any comments?

When To Use What for Testing

As mentioned before, when it comes to testing in SharePoint, your options are very limited. I am able to share a few items with you, but the odds of you having to perform manual testing for at least parts of your project will be very high. Here are a few ideas on testing different types of solutions in SharePoint:

- Add-in Model: Visual Studio Team Services
- Full-trust Solutions: Visual Studio Team Services
- JavaScript (on page or off page): Try tools such as Jasmine, Phantom.js or Mochas

*Note: I have not used Jasmine, Phantom.js or Mocha nor have I heard of anyone using them. However, they should allow the ability to create automated scripts that mimic the behavior of a human and save time from repetitive manual tasks. I have heard that they require a fair amount of time to setup and the costs are possibly high. This is something you will have to investigate.

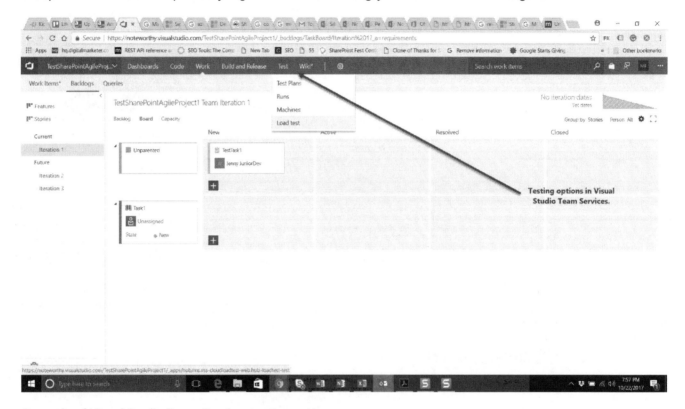

Example of Visual Studio Team Services testing options.

Regression Testing

Regression testing is a type of software testing which verifies that software which was previously developed and tested still performs the same way after it was changed or interfaced with other software. Changes may include software enhancements, patches, configuration changes, etc. One issue is that setting up ongoing regression testing for SharePoint is difficult. Unless you can figure out a way to program automated scripts to mimic user behaviors that can be used as repeatable process (see some suggestions above on software to do this), you will end up having to do regression testing manually. For a long, ongoing project that has many phases, this can end up being very painful and time consuming unfortunately. In the real world, I admit I have seen many companies completely skip regression testing which is not a good thing.

User Acceptance Testing vs. Unit Testing

Unit tests are created by programmers or occasionally by white box testers during the development process. User acceptance testing (UAT) is the last phase of the software testing process. During UAT, actual software users test the software to make sure it can handle required tasks in real-world scenarios, according to specifications.

Finding Your Guinea Pigs

If you have properly done a stakeholder assessment in the beginning of the project, you should most likely know who will be good candidates to perform your UAT. I will seek out the persons who will end up using the site on the most regular basis as well as business manager stakeholders to perform UAT. In some cases, if there is a stakeholder who happens to be extra excited about the project, I might try to include them in the UAT process as well.

Project Wrap-Up

Rollout and Signoff

To wrap up this chapter I wanted to review some of the final steps I take when wrapping up a project after it has passed testing and been successfully deployed into production.

- I ensure that I get a final signoff on the project deliverable so that any billings can start to begin (if the project was based on successful delivery or fixed bid).
- I set up a person to maintain the adoption process as time progresses and the things they will do to ensure the project doesn't turn into a "graveyard".
- I create and give the client a *Transition Document* to explain everything that has happened on the site, any requirements that were not met as specified, where to find documentation regarding how the site works and made sure if I have coded anything there are notes documenting how the code works. If you have created a SharePoint project portal as listed in the chapter in *Building Your SharePoint Project,* I will make sure to upload most of these files there and make sure the stakeholders are aware of the project site.
- If possible, I like to send out an anonymous survey to the persons involved in the project to gather feedback on what they felt went right and what could have been done better. Using a tool such as Microsoft Forms is great for this purpose.

Regarding taking notes on what did and what didn't work. This is how I came up with the majority of content for this book and my questionnaire. Every project is a learning experience, just try to make the next project a better one than what you have done before.

Sign on the Dotted Line!

Now that you have delivered everything, have your UAT documents to back-up your functional requirements were met and your users are working with the site, you may need to get sign-off to receive payment (this applies to internal departments at times and external consultants). Ironically, after working feverishly, bending over backwards and going above and beyond expectation to provide SharePoint solutions for some clients, getting them to finally sign-off on the project can be challenging. I am not sure if there is a fear they have that they will continue to need more changes and don't have the budget or what the specific reasoning is admittedly. However, in these cases, I will give a couple of friendly reminders and then may have to resort to threatening to disable the site or going to other stakeholders for assistance. I personally would ask around to other managers or stakeholders first before resorting to disabling a site, but there was one non-SharePoint site I worked on many years ago where it did come down to turning a site off for lack of payment.

9. OTHER SHAREPOINT ODDS & ENDS

Tips for Working With "Challenging" People
- The "know it all"
  - I try never to come across as "knowing more than someone", it doesn't work. If you have an issue with someone who constantly challenges everything you are suggesting in SharePoint, back it up with evidence either via a demo or articles from the Microsoft website.
- Getting people that are too busy or uninterested to respond
  - I have definitely had stakeholders not get back in a timely fashion. A couple of ideas I have used over the years is sending a status with a big red bar showing it past due or even politely mentioning due to budget concerns we will have to disable the site until it has been properly approved.
- Wants to control everything
  - Working with someone who wants to control everything and is constantly breathing down your neck is no fun. Earning their trust by showing your SharePoint skills and aligning your vision to theirs could help in this situation.
- The developer who's no longer there
  - Unfortunately many projects you pick up might be left-overs from past SharePoint consultants. The reality is that most developers and administrators do not leave detailed notes and documentation (mostly to keep job security). There isn't much you can do other than starting to reverse engineer what you find. One note, try not to blame everything on the previous consultant or it may come across as you not being able to solve problems which is why you hired (most likely.)

Hiring SharePoint Talent
Personally, I am a bit less formal when interviewing potential candidates for SharePoint job openings. The reality of things these days is that everyone uses the internet to find samples of code and answers to their questions. Although I may ask some specific technical questions, I try to ask how they would handle a situation or ask for examples of difficult technical experiences they have faced and how they found the answers to resolve the challenge. If you know you have a specific need, for example you may need to hire someone to setup oAuth to create an open-source authentication mechanism across SharePoint and another site, I could understand asking more specific question regarding this technically.

SharePoint Business Analyst Interview Questions
Since this book is specifically targeted toward SharePoint business analysts, I wanted to give some examples of hiring questions you may face or may need to study from or use should you be looking to hire someone for this position. Here are some samples below:

Do you have any certifications in SharePoint?
What are some business solutions you have created with SharePoint? How were you able to determine there was a gap and that SharePoint was the best solution for it?

How do you keep up with SharePoint's constant change and the ongoing, continuous learning in IT.

How do you determine the best way to plan out or architect a SharePoint project. As an example, when you would you use a list over a library?

Have you done any work with adoption or governance?

Explain some of the meetings you have had with stakeholders and the different topics you have discussed with them. How did you get from "an idea" to a finalized SharePoint project placed into production?

How have you dealt with difficult stakeholders in the past, provide an example.

Name some types of documentation and / or methodologies you have used to gather requirements for SharePoint projects. Do you have any favorite software you use to accomplish this?

What experience do you have managing, configuring, applying security to and training users with SharePoint sites?

RFPs / RFIs

When a company, organization, or federal agency is in need of SharePoint assistance, it is common for them to issue what is called an Request for Proposal (RFP) as part of the procurement. The purpose of issuing the RFP is often to get vendors bidding to win the work and to gain insight into how different offerors would approach their technical needs. It gives vendors a chance to not only showcase their SharePoint experience and skills, but to also give a pricing proposal.

Proposal writing is known to be very stressful because there are tight deadlines, and require extreme attention to detail. Every question and requirement must be answered. Also, there are sometimes very specific rules about the formatting of the document. Some companies or organizations even throw in small unique formatting requirements just to see if the offerors are paying attention to detail! A common practice when beginning to work on a proposal is to go through the requirements and questions with a fine-tooth comb and document them in a spreadsheet so you can check them off as you write and review your work. In bigger companies there are usually several levels of review before submitting proposals. A proposal expert once told me that he believes that he wins so many proposals simply because he pays such close attention to the formatting requirements.

The basic components of a proposal vary depending on the type of request but there are some constants. A cover letter is written introducing the offeror and summarizing what their services consist of. Also, a page including the names, address, point of contact, and contact information of the company is required. An important section of the proposal will include the experience of the company and how it relates to the work needed. Offerors are also often required to provide key personnel for the work along with their resumes. Management styles, employee retention objectives, quality control, software development styles and scheduling are also key components to the proposal. Infographics that are simple and visually appealing are very helpful. For SharePoint proposals the technical approach for how the team will meet or better yet exceed the expectations is the second most important piece of information. The most important piece is usually the price.

Proposal writing requires a very specific skill set and is a task that many SharePoint business analysts participate in. The range of participation varies greatly. Some SharePoint business analysts may only provide technical advisory on how the company would respond to the requirements. Others may write the entire proposal including searching for qualified resources within their firm to list as key personnel and developing the pricing model. Having proposal writing skills comes in handy to the SharePoint business analyst when they do not have any technical work and need a productive activity.

Analytics

Analytics for SharePoint mostly fall into 3 options:

1. Built-in analytics found in site settings - these are limited in functionality, however they can provide some basic information. Admittedly, most organizations I have worked at have not found the built-in analytics SharePoint offers to be enough for them to fulfill their business needs. This is why I will list the next 3 options.
2. Google Analytics – Almost every organization I have worked at uses Google Analytics. They will usually alter the SharePoint master page for the site collections to include the tracking code and use Google's portal to review the results. I realize this isn't a Microsoft product, but I am speaking from real-world experiences and this is what I have seen used more than any other product.
3. Third party analytics products made for or compatible with SharePoint. There are only a few on the market I know of at this time. Since I am not endorsing any of them, I would suggest you go to your favorite search engine and search for them. They are not free so you will have to determine if they are within the budget you have and will fulfill your business needs for recording analytical SharePoint data.

10. SAMPLE SHAREPOINT REQUIREMENT TEMPLATES

NOTE: Samples of these documents in Word or Excel formats are available for download from my website <u>with a proof of purchase</u>. I realize printing these pages from an eBook reader might not format them properly.

Visit http://www.matthewjbailey.com/sharepoint-business-analyst/

1. SharePoint Requirements "Conversation Starter" Questionnaire
2. Stakeholder Document
3. Business Case Document
4. Functional Specification Document
5. Field Data Type Document
6. 3rd Party Intranet Questionnaire
7. Statement of Work (SOW)
8. Architectural Proposal (Provider Hosted Add-In)

SharePoint "Conversation Starter" Requirements Questionnaire

Author: Matthew J. Bailey

www.matthewjbailey.com

REMOVE THIS PAGE BEFORE USING IN PRODUCTION

Project Name

Company / Organization

Version:

Last Updated:

Updated By:

1. Instructions and Overview of this Document
1.1 REMOVE THIS PAGE BEFORE USING IT IN PRODUCTION

This page is meant as a quick guide on how to use the document, it is not meant to remain after you started using the document for an actual project. You will probably want to delete it and other information you find that is not relevant to the project you are working on.

1.2 Target Audience for this Document

Anyone who works with SharePoint that needs to organize, create, manage or architect a SharePoint project. The document is mainly targeted at SharePoint business analysts, however developers, project managers and administrators may find value in it as well.

1.3 Instructions for this Document

The document is organized into sections regarding different parts of SharePoint that you may need depending on the type of SharePoint project you are working on. As mentioned above, there are a lot of sections on the document and most likely you will not need to use them all at the same time. Take what you need and remove the other parts, saving the original unaltered template for reuse on the next project. I have tried to add a few examples in places of what types of why you would want to ask the questions you are asking. To update the footer, use the tools in the ribbon in Word or double click in the footer area.

1.4 Purpose of Document

The document is a "conversation starter" and checklist for a SharePoint project. It is **not** a:

- Official requirement document
- Functional requirement document
- Technical specification document
- UAT (Testing script) document
- Flow diagram
- Data type diagram
- Design mockup / guide

If needed, you should create these documents separately or added them as appendixes to the document.

2. Environment

Specifically, detail the SharePoint environment you will be working in so that you know what features and options you will have to work with and be able to do.

* As some companies have hybrid or comingled environments, you may end up selecting more than one option in this section.

2.1 Edition (s)

	Office 365 Development Tenant
	Office 365 Business
	Office 365 Business Essentials
	Office 365 Business Premium
	Office 365 ProPlus
	Office 365 Enterprise E1
	Office 365 Enterprise E3
	Office 365 Enterprise E5
	Office 365 Enterprise K1
	Office 365 U.S. Government Community G1
	Office 365 U.S. Government Community G3
	Office 365 U.S. Government Community G5
	SharePoint Online managed tenant (like Office 365 but Microsoft manages it and does not update like Office 365 does)
	SharePoint 2016 Standard & Office Web Apps Servers
	SharePoint 2016 Standard & Office Web Apps Servers
	SharePoint 2016 Enterprise
	SharePoint 2016 Enterprise
	SharePoint 2013 Foundation
	SharePoint 2013 Standard
	SharePoint 2013 Enterprise
	SharePoint 2010 Foundation
	SharePoint 2010 Standard
	SharePoint 2010 Enterprise
	SharePoint 2007 Enterprise
	SharePoint 2007 Standard
	WSS 3.0
	SharePoint 2003
	Other version _____

2.2 Configuration

	100% on-premises
	100% Cloud (not VMs in cloud, Office 365 cloud)
	Hybrid (*explain*)

2.3 Service Applications Enabled

	Application Management Service
	SharePoint Translation Services
	Access Services 2010
	Access Services
	Business Data Connectivity service
	Excel Services Application
	Managed Metadata service
	PerformancePoint Service Application
	Search service
	Secure Store Service
	State service
	Usage and Health Data Collection service
	User Profile service
	Visio Graphics Service
	Word Automation Services
	Other _____
	Other _____
	Other _____
	Other _____
	Other _____
	Other _____

2.4 Development / Administration Tools Allowed

	Visual Studio
	Visual Studio Code
	SharePoint Designer
	InfoPath Designer
	PowerApps
	Flow

	PowerShell ISE
	Other _____
	Other _____
	Other _____

2.5 Development Methods Allowed

	Full Trust Solutions (on-premises servers only)
	Provider Hosted Add-In (app)
	SharePoint Hosted Add-in (app)
	Client Side Scripting
	Page Layout Customizations
	Master Page Changes Allowed
	Other _____
	Other _____

2.6 Third Party Server Based Addons / Software Purchased

	Nintex
	Metalogix
	ShareGate
	K2
	Other _____
	Other _____

You may need to contact your farm administrator to have some of these questions answered, they may or may not be resistant in sharing the information with you. Explain to them you would like to know so that you as you are planning out SharePoint solutions, you will be aware of what you can and cannot do thus saving time and money. If they will not share the information with you, fell free to give them my name and I will argue with them for you □. Hey, I used to be a SharePoint Administrator too, and there is really no valid reason of why they should not be sharing the architecture, configuration, tools purchased or services available within your organization. You are not asking for passwords or other highly secure information

3. Stakeholders

The image below is an example of my stakeholder assessment document. **Please use this separate document that should be included in your sample templates.**

3.1 Example of a stakeholder assessment form.

- *Are all parties who will be using the site from managers, editors to visitors involved in the meetings? Are there other departments who interact with this site or who have data in it that need to be present? Are there managers who must approve anything and should attend?*
- *Would sitting with the people who use this on a daily basis help create the requirements?*
- *Have you included any IT, other project managers, other SharePoint developers or governance board members who could affect*
- *The last column asks the "what's in it for me" question, what do they need to get out of this SharePoint project*

4. Site Purpose & Business Need

Why do you want and need to move to SharePoint?

What do you want people to think when they see and use the finished site / SharePoint project?

Can this statement be validated with a delivered SharePoint site/project to mark the project or phase as "successful and completed"?

Examples:
- *To provide guidance and recent news updates to our entire company regarding what our team is working on and the services our team provides.*
- *To allow users to request specific items by submitting a list of detailed information regarding about their need (a new laptop, a new site, a new resource, a repair, etc.)*
- *The site is a mission critical.*
- *To replace an existing system that is not meeting our needs and has these GAPs: _____ (when did you move to this system, were there systems before that?). What went wrong with the system you are using now along the way?*
- *There are specific tedious, time consuming tasks that we have to do currently and we want to improve our business process and time spent*
- *Performance on our current system is poor*
- *We need to version and remove documents for historic purposes*
- *We need to create a news and project collaboration site for a global HR department where we can keep people aware of events, news stories, encourage discussions, display photos and create a sense of community. The previous site we had lacked user engagement.*
- *What is the end goal, to engage users, create lead generation, make documents/publications available to users?*

Bad Examples:
- *Someone told us SharePoint was cool so we just thought we should start putting everything in it without a plan.*

4.1 Questions to Help Identify the Business Purpose & Need

4.1.1 Has Anything Been Done to Solve This Problem Already?

Sometimes there have already been attempted solutions on to fix a business problem that have occurred prior to you being called into a SharePoint project. In one example, an organization was using hundreds of Excel files to track information amongst multiple teams to track items. Asking questions such as this could help extract some of the major pain points that the stakeholders are trying to avoid from happening again when building this in SharePoint.

4.1.2 What Do You Need (Most) From Me?

We can bring a lot of expectations to our roles – templates we think need filling out, specifications we'd like to create, and models we'd like to draw. But sometimes what our stakeholders need is different from what we want to provide them. And sometimes what they think they need and what they *really* need are very different. The answer to this question gets you information about what they think they need so you can either start fulfilling their expectations directly or starting the process of resetting their expectations about what you'll be doing as the business analyst.

As You Are Getting Into the Details

4.1.3 Can You Give Me an Example?

If you sense you are not getting the whole story, ask this question. Asking for an example or many examples to represent different requirements can help expand the conversation and ensure your requirements cover all the scenarios.

What Problem Are We Trying to Solve?

This question often must be asked multiple times to get to the real answer and it also must be asked with finesse so that it doesn't generate conflict. Click here to find 10 ways to discover what the problem really is.

In my experience, most conflict and significant stakeholder project disagreements result from either a difference in business goals (which you'll discover by getting to the root of the problem) or a terminology misunderstanding. And that's the topic of our next question.

4.1.4 What Does That Mean?

Resolving misunderstandings in terminology is an area where a business analyst can demonstrate strong leadership skills. This question often leads a discussion where stakeholders share their different definitions, begin clarifying each other's definitions, and offering up examples of negative cases to clarify the definition. This type of discussion often leads to at least a few "aha" moments – for you and everyone else.

Ask questions about acronyms, confusing terms, and organization-specific phrases. And don't overlook the obvious and generic terms like customer, order, or issue as often they have the most false assumptions surrounding their meaning. Since these terms seem so obvious, often no one has bothered to ask what they mean in a long, long time.

As You Are Closing a Discussion

4.1.5 Is There Anything We Didn't Discuss?

Use this question and variations of it whenever you can – between agenda items, at the end of a meeting, and before finalizing a requirements specification. Once your stakeholders get into the habit of you asking them for their questions, they'll get better at filling in gaps and providing more relevant information.

4.1.6 Is There Any Reason We Can't Move Forward?

While the previous set of questions are more open-ended in nature, this question creates a sense of urgency that gets your stakeholders to commit to the next step. Used at the end of the meeting or when finalizing a deliverable, this question ensures that sign-off really means sign-off.

5. Use Case / User Stories

#	Type	Category	Use / User	Category (viewing, editing, adding)	Story / Case	Need vs. Nice-to-have	Comments

Include:
- *Action needed to complete*
- *Viewing restrictions (during before and after events)*
- *Submission restrictions (during before and after events)*
- *Editing restrictions (during before and after events)*

* You may need to add an addendum to this document or reference your use cases and user stories in another document as they can be graphical or long in description

Story: As a _____ *(role of person)*, I want to be able to _____*(function of the system)*, so that _____ *(goal)* can be achieved.

Case:

- *Sunny Day vs. Rainy Day use cases, how will this be dealt with when things go wrong?*
- *Use Cases are meant to provide such a formalized blueprint of the project that they often leave little room for negotiation or project additions. No right or wrong answer, open for growth yet that growth can cause project issues and scope creep.*

6. User Roles of the Site / Security Architecture

User Role	SharePoint Level of Permission	Custom Permission Level or OOTB	Applicable to which parts of site (s)	Who would be in this group/role?		

- *Who is the audience of the site?*
- *How many different "roles" of this site will there be and what should each role be able to do? (i.e., Full Control, editors, read only/visitors)*
- *Will there be any special security restrictions on some content such as certain libraries/lists, specific documents, folders (even though not recommended) or even specific columns that should not be viewable to some users? Should people be able to only edit their own content? (lists easy to do, libraries not as much).*
- *Is there any restriction on who can view vs. edit and does that change based on a state of the process (i.e. after this happened, no one but the Admin can edit the bottom half of the form).*
- *All one site collection shared within another site collection, subsites?*
- *Is there any restriction on certain people seeing certain things (audiences) or some people editing vs. reading and at different states*
- *Is search to not show certain things within the site or within a global search result (like a company- wide search server)*

7. Site Setup / Architecture / Data Migration

- Will there need to be any data migration or importing from other sources to populate lists, lookups, or data before the site goes live or is a process that happens on a regular basis? Is this a one or two-way import/export process?
- If there is a migration, will the size of the data being migrated (total size of all files, size of some files being larger than 2GB or number of items) be an issue with SP limits?
- What is the average file size of documents? (Office 365 2 GB "advertised" limit, more behind scenes, on-premises different per company)
- Will the number of items in a list or library or size of uploads over time create an issue? (get examples of data sizes or number of items.)
- Will the overall site size be an issue? (mega site-collections in Office 365)
- Are you going to be creating a flat site architecture (meaning site collections with no sub-sites or one large site collection with many sub-sites? Make sure to check the Microsoft website for size and item limits if you have large amounts of data, many fine-grained permissions (security scopes) or many complex workflows as to not go over the software boundaries.

8. Document/Object Management/Storage

Numbers of, file sizes and types of artifacts being placed in this site(s):

Document

Video

Photo

Will you be using any of these:
- Document versioning
- content approval
- Check-out controls in SharePoint 2013 (publishing)
- Custom content types

Will you be using and of the following to manage objects/documents/items:
- Records management
- eDiscovery
- Information rights management
- Archiving

More information at: https://technet.microsoft.com/en-us/library/cc263266.aspx

9. Viewing & Retrieving Data

Note: each need for a role/user to view or obtain data can be a use case/user story

Needs to display, sort, access, search & retrieve artifacts (metadata, folders, views, search)

- Search
  - Metadata filters
  - Multimedia search
  - Result sources
  - Query transformations
  - Search drop downs on pages need to be customized? Search center issues/universal search center
- Views
  - Drop down or link to find specific docs
  - Personal views
  - Audience targeting views

- Dynamic / Multiple sources / Rollups
  - Example of connected web parts retrieving all related info
  - CSWP
  - (Sliders) Text based rollups vs. rich-text Where should you click on what to go to where?

9.1 Views

View Name	Columns Included	Special Formula?	Filter Criteria	Sorting	Other Notes

9.2 Search Configurations

Refiner	Single or Multi							

10. User Engagement

- How will people find your site?
- What should be on the home page as the most important and engaging?
- How can you engage the user?
- What do you want visitors to do once they are at your site?
- Short term and long term goals for the site?
- Alerts on lists, workflow triggers, subscribing to feeds, likes, community contributors, gamification?
- Is Google Analytics or some other type of tracking software needed or used at this organization? *Built in SharePoint reporting is rather limited.*

10.1 Social Interaction & Collaboration

Newsfeeds
Blogging
Tagging
Discussions

11. Graphical Design

Do any of the following apply?

- Must always use certain fonts?
- Website pages, lists, views, menus, images must be responsive and display properly on.. (iphone 4, 5, Android, IE 8-11, etc.). Make sure requirement document has graphical mockups of each format or decide you are using Bootstrap or something)
- Views have a more artistic display (use JSLink, CQWP, display templates)
- Do list items or pages in libraries need to look a specific way other than how they appear "OOTB" with their design?
- Mobile friendly/responsive required?
- Is there a design guide? If so, location?
- Are there already design elements pushed to every site including custom code that could interfere with development (i.e. every site already has a specific version of jQuery in it from a design being used and would any new programming you add be dependent on it or affect it)

Mockup #	Object of Mockup	Appendix Reference #	Who Will Design?	Complete?

11.1 User Friendly Design / Audience

Who are the owners and users of this site from a technical or position of power? Do things need to be very intuitive with little explanation or is the audience used to working with SharePoint (rollout / adoption plan)

 Help section (customized help site collection, an editable FAQ page, a discussion section, etc)

 Site contacts for assistance

 Feedback/suggestions

 Mission statement

12. Data Submission, Editing & Viewing

12.1 Forms

- Mandatory fields
- Field types (people picker? Especially if going to have "my views". Lookup (to where?), choice, check, multi-line text, etc. - remember how InfoPath alters so much of this)
- Special validation of data type (one value based on another, % can't be lower or higher than 100, dates, SSI or CC numbers, certain dates are not allowed to be before or after other dates, data conversion of something entered, etc.)
- Dates international format (or if not possible put a label next to them since controlled on server)
- Will fields that are choice need to be updated by the site owner later as needed (InfoPath issues)?
- Will this form in general want to be changed by the end user later by themselves?
- Will their need to be a message that appears after the form is submitted
- Is there any auto sequence numbering needed
- Will the form need to go to a certain location after it is submitted
- Will parts of the form need to be locked or only show to certain users based on different steps in a process?
- Will there need to be attachments uploaded?
- Help or tips/lables for how the form should be filled in? (i.e., what goes in this field)
- Dynamic rows like more show up based on if you need more to fill in
- Back buttons - what happens (especially with InfoPath)

12.2 Web & Site Content Management

Multiple environments (authoring, staging, production) / cross-site publishing
Managed navigation (metadata), site settings, text file or something else
Metadata planning: term sets, terms, etc. https://technet.microsoft.com/en-us/library/ee530389.aspx

13. Business Process Automation / Workflows

Business Process Mapping & Visio processes or diagrams?

Will this site/project include any workflows?

Will they have mail integration/notifications/ group mailboxes (*being deprecated*)

14. User Management & Functionality

1. Pages must be editable in a form based concept where a non-technical user can enter and edit information on all lists, libraries, pages & menus. Exceptions to this rule might include (a unique JavaScript carousel or modal pop-up menu that is managed in a text file)
2. Menus - remember the issues with the IT Delivery online site where the Edit Links showed to everyone with contributor, but using CSS to hide it hid her groups. But she needed a drop down menu so had to use term store. Another issue was using term store menus in sibling site with ticket we opened to Microsoft and how it broke another site if you used it somewhere else. Also, issues like someone having multiple sites like OLS and their 4 site collections, do you just have a simple link for "go back home" or how do you manage 5 term store menus unless they will let you publish it as a managed metadata service term set

14.1 Accessibility & Language

1. Foreign languages (variations, language packs, machine translation, importing translated files):
   o https://technet.microsoft.com/en-us/library/ff628966.aspx https://technet.microsoft.com/en-us/library/cc262404.aspx
2. Public facing, disability or accessibility requirements
3. Mobile access https://technet.microsoft.com/en-us/library/gg610510.aspx

15. Wireframing

Content of each page, web part zones (if using page layouts), dynamic rotation of last 3 items or based on dates, sections above for each page.

16. Build / Testing & Launch Plan Questions

* This section is NOT meant to be a total replacement of a build, testing or launch document, it is just some questions to think about and ask.

Instructions for site owners? Where are they stored, in a common place, employee turnover is fact of life

17. Deliverables / Final wrap

- Timelines, Budget & Process: Is there a standard cost for an assessment and is that the first step? Is that to present a quote to the user? Mention any costs of additional per user/license, project based and ongoing maintenance.
- What are you expectations of the final deliverable, in general? For example, managing the site you want to be able to change which types of things and
- Training docs of what type
- Training sessions (is there basic SharePoint training needed, or special training for nuances & customizations
- ions on the specific project you are doing? Does the user know how to do basic SharePoint things such as add CEWP? Spelling/Grammar, special terms that a certain team only uses)
- Data import
- Security final steps
- Change management dates notified in advance
- Launch dates / deadlines (hard or soft) & budgetary constraints

18. Governance / Change Team Process?

Worries about getting things into production that should be addressed upfront - approvals from legal, change management boards, production freezes,

Legal team issues, may vary per country

19.1 Governance

1. Will there be user submitted content that needs to be moderated? (discussions, newsfeeds, new user requests, standards)
2. Legal - does the site have to have a terms and conditions or a user sign off, does legal allow blog sites, if a user is an outside contractor will rules of what they can do be different?
3. Is there a delay in getting a site provisioned (i.e. a request tool in Azure that someone has to approve or budget that needs to get approved and signed off/returned)

THE SHAREPOINT BUSINESS ANALYST GUIDE

19. In Scope / Out of Scope

This project will NOT include:

Things that were not in budget or schedule

Things that were turned off by IT or not allowed to be used

Etc

__NOTE:__ All scope changes will require a scope change document and will be decided to either be added into the current project at no additional cost, with additional cost, without additional time needed, without additional time needed or placed into a future phase of the project.

20. Risks

Examples of risks might be:
- *Not having multiple environments for dev, stage and prod could cause issues with having to deploy live code fixes and enhancements*
- *Not being given test IDs to use, especially in the case of multiple users playing different roles*
- *Backup & restore considerations*

21. Timelines for Project

- Cut off for an RFP or if no RFP cut off for no more requirements
- Test dates and people who will do this
- Production rollout freezes
- How will the project be managed to stay on schedule? Tasks, managed somewhere with project, teams, VS Team Studio, tasks in a box, etc.

22. Technical Specifications - Content Types (forms / data capture)

Order #	Column Name	Data Type (*See choices below....*)	Required (Y/N)	Entry Validation (date or certain format like SSN, max # chars, calculated)	If choice, checkbox or metadata: choices to pick from	Helper text *(additional description)*	Indexed (performance)	Conditional (based on another field or object/action)	Notes: (i.e., certain fields security changes, visibility,etc.)
1.									
2.									
3.									
4.									
5.									

Single line of text
Multiple lines of text
Choice (menu to choose from)
Number (1, 1.0, 100)
Currency ($, ¥, €)
Date and Time
Lookup (information already on this site)
Yes/No (check box)
Person or Group
Hyperlink or Picture
Calculated (calculation based on other columns)
Task Outcome
External Data
Managed Metadata

22. Monitoring

Will search reports, reporting, barcodes or other IRM features be needed

23. Information Architecture & Structure of Content

Grouping by: department or date or ? size limits threshold issues and what makes sense for the users of the system

PAGE INTENTIONALLY LEFT BLANK

Stakeholder Assessment Document

Stakehol der Name	Stakeho lder's Contact Informa tion	How much impact does this person have on the project?	How much influence does this stakeholder have over the project?	What is this stakeholder getting from this project?	What role & responsibil ities will this stakeholde r have?	What could this stakeholder do to cause an issue with your project?	What is your plan on keeping this stakeholder engaged?
Henrietta HumanR esource Manager	hhr@fa kecomp any.com	High - She should be consider ed project sponsor	High	A new image to project to the company about the HR department. A new, more modern way to communicat e with other HR employees.	Approving the design. Approving the site structure and site functionalit y.	Change their mind far too often, need signoff on approvals.	Send weekly updates and demos to show progress. Ask for feedback occassionally to see how she feels the project is going.
Cathy Commun icator	cc@fake compan y.com	Medium - co-author of site	Low - Henrietta didn't seem to think Cathy's opinion mattered much unfortunatel y.	A way to communicat e to the organization items happening in her division of human resources.	Authoring content in one section of the site.	Complain a lot possibly. Not complete her section of the site content.	Send updates only when something affects her portion of the site. Have a training meeting on how to use the site to encourage her to complete the rest on her own.
Andy ITAdmin	aa@fak ecompa ny.com	High - if he does not deploy site we are at a stand still	Low - Henrietta has too much clout with executives to allow Andy to be a roadblock.	Standard job responsibiliti es.	Deploying the site to production.	Not deploy the site.	Give Andy updates on project dates to make sure he will be available on deployment day.

Patty Project Manager	ppm@fakecompany.com	Medium - in charge of budgeting, timelines and people related to project.	Medium - Patty could bring up issues that could move their way up the pipeline of employees or mark the project on her status reports as not going well.	Credit for the project being deployed successfully.	Budgeting, timelines and people related to project.	Mark the project on her status reports as not going well.	Daily updates on where we are at with the project plan, any potential issues being discovered, stakeholders not being as engaged as they should be, etc.

*Remember, electronic copies of this document in Excel (which display much better) are available for a free download from my website with proof of purchase. Please visit http://www.matthewjbailey.com/sharepoint-business-analyst/

*The people listed in this document in blue are examples, please delete them before using this document in production.

PAGE INTENTIONALLY LEFT BLANK

_____ Project: Business Case

Organization/Company Name here

Version:

Status:

Last Updated:

Updated By:

1.0 Executive Summary

Depending on the length of the business case you may want to include a high-level summary of the project. Although it appears as the first section of the business case, it should be the last written after understanding everything involved with the project.

This should be a short summary of the entire business case.

1.1 ROI Validation

Return on investment, or ROI, is the ratio of a profit or loss made in a fiscal year expressed in terms of an investment and shown as a percentage of increase or decrease in the value of the investment during the fiscal year and possibly future fiscal years. The basic formula for ROI is:

ROI = Saved Amount from Project Returns / Total Investment * 100.

Since SharePoint is about automating business processes and collaboration, I have used the term Saved Amount from Project Returns instead of the word "profit". If SharePoint had been created as an e-Commerce software, perhaps profit would apply. However, in almost all cases SharePoint is about reducing costs (via time, man hours, frustrations, improved organization, mismanaged or lost artifacts, etc.)

1.2 Alternate Outcomes & Effects

This section looks at alternative futures by measuring the impact on project outcomes or assumptions of changing values in which there is uncertainty. It also can describe the financial impact of not doing a project.

2.0 Project Definition

The most intensive part of the business case: for the project sponsors(s), stakeholders, and project team members.

It should explain most of the why, what, and how regarding your project.

2.1 Background Information

Gives a clear introduction to the business case and project. Contains a brief overview of the reasons why the project or business change has come about: the problem, opportunity, or change of circumstances.

2.2 Business Objective

Describes why are you doing the project. The business objective answers the following questions:
- *What is your goal?*
- *What is needed to overcome the problem?*
- *How will the project support the business strategy?*

2.3 Benefits and Limitations

Describes the financial and non-financial benefits of this project. It should explain why you need a project.

Example: By saving an assistant 4 hours each work week manually completing papers, copying them and distributing them by hand, SharePoint's electronic list form will replace this time consuming task and allow faster tracking and sharing.

2.4 Solution Identification

Identify the potential solutions to the problem and describe them in enough detail for the reader to understand. This may include alternatives to creating the solution in SharePoint or even not identifying a viable solution at all.

2.5 Timeline & Plan Overview

Project schedule and brief summary of tasks involved and stakeholder responsible to accomplish project completion.

2.6 Risk Assessment

The risk assessment summarizes the significant risks and opportunities and how they are managed. The risks included should cover those that could arise from you project or the organization's ability to deliver change.

This section answers the following questions:

- *What risks are involved?*

- *What are the consequences of a risk happening?*

- *What opportunities may emerge?*

- *What plans are in place to deal with the risks?*

2.7 Project Approach & Methodology

Describers how the plan to pursue the project would be pursued and created.

Example: The project will be built using consulting company "A" who will provide 3 SharePoint developers. These developers will work with our internal SharePoint business analyst and SharePoint administrator using an Agile methodology to deliver the project.

Credits: *Portions of this document were adapted from WorkFront's Business Case Template. Feel free to check them out at:* https://resources.workfront.com/project-management-blog/how-to-write-a-business-case-4-steps-to-a-perfect-business-case-template

PAGE INTENTIONALLY LEFT BLANK

Functional Specification Document

Organization/Company Name here

Version:

Status:

Last Updated:

Updated By:

Document Information and Revision History

Project Name:	

Revision History

Date	Editor	Version	Description of Change

Distribution

The document has been distributed to:

Name	Title	Date of Issue	Version

Document Location

The source of the document is located in:

_____

Purpose of Document

Example: The purpose of this document is to define the functional and non-functional requirements for a defined project or change request. This document should be used as a guide/checklist to help ensure that requirements are well thought out, documented and approved prior to investing development and deployment resources. It is the responsibility of the Project Manager to ensure that requirements get document by the Project Team and reviewed and approved by the project's defined Governing Body.

Introduction

Purpose

Example: This document describes the requirements for the _____ system moving off of the file shares/servers and into a website so that end users can find media files more easily and longer term more customized features might be built in regarding file status and custom security.

Requirements Management Approach

Example: These requirements must be reviewed and approved by those listed in the approvers section. After approval of this document, changes will be reviewed and prioritized by the Project Manager.

Intended Audience and Reading Suggestions

Example: This document is intended to be read by developers, business technical analysts, and project managers involved in the migration project.

Business Benefits

Business Benefit	Supporting Features	Acceptance Criteria

This section describes the rationale of the requirements being specified, including relevant benefits, objectives, and goals. Relate the product or solution to corporate goals or business strategies, if possible. If a separate vision and scope document is available, refer to it rather than duplicating its contents here. Describe how the benefits will be achieved by the features outlined in this document and how those features will be verified for acceptance.

References

Document Title	Description	Document Location (e.g. Peregrine, DMC, etc.)	Author

Overall Description

Product Functions

This section summarizes the major functions the product must perform or must let the user perform in order to fulfill the requested requirements.

In Scope Functions

	In Scope
2.1.1.1	
2.1.1.2	
2.1.1.3	
2.1.1.4	
2.1.1.5	

Out of Scope Functions

	Out of Scope
2.1.2.1	
2.1.2.2	
2.1.2.3	
2.1.2.4	
2.1.2.5	

Examples of In scope requirements:

- *different levels of security for site as outlined in requirement #107*
- *The ability to upload up to 2 GB files. Other factors such as network latency, a user's computer can affect this at times.*
- *Ability for the site owner to manage the meta data / keywords for the site*

Examples of out of scope requirements:

Once a file is uploaded to the site it will be considered "live", there will not be any "draft" or "final" status assigned to each file.

- *Community Site for this phase of the project*
- *Creation of an approval workflow*
- *Integration with any system*
- *Ability to edit a non-office based document*
- *Ability to upload exe or any other non approved file type*
- *There will be no preview for .zip files in search.*
- *Mobile responsive content author experience*
- *The site will be responsive from a display mode only, meaning that content authors wont have a responsive design to upload content but users of the site will see the site in a mobile-adaptive responsive design.*
- *Once a file is uploaded to the site it will be considered "live", there will not be any "draft" or "final" status assigned to each file.*

Operating Environment

Examples of design and implementation constraints:

- *Updates will be made in SharePoint 2013 (Office 365 Dedicated) for all team sites.*

Design and Implementation Constraints

Examples of design and implementation constraints:

- *Development and deployment must adhere to the restrictions of our hosted Office 365 Dedicated - SharePoint 2013 environment*

Assumptions and Dependencies

Examples of assumptions and dependencies:

- *Any changes required after delivery and acceptance of solution will require a new SOW.*
- *Requesting team is responsible for all end user documentation, training and communications*
- *SharePoint team is not responsible for establishing, enforcing or communicating acceptable compliance use policies or statements per compliance requirements regarding information privacy.*
- *All file size estimates given from business stakeholder were given as "best effort", however we realize there are other factors that may occur over the next year regarding if the site will become as large as it is planned for or not.*

Functional Requirements

Summary

Req #	Priority	Description

Individual Requirement Details

Req #	Category	Description	Owner	Comments
3.2.1				
3.2.2				
3.2.3				

Examples of functional requirements (*REMEMBER – we want these be as detailed as possible to avoid confusion!!!)

Design   The site will follow the design demonstrated in Appendix A using the xxxxx theme to ensure it follows the same branding guidelines as the rest of the intranet.   Adoption Team

Design will be inherited from the existing theme named _____ that already is applied to the organization's intranet site

Development List based slider will be created and used on the homepage of the site. The slider will be controlled from a list that end users can change out the text, which items appear in the slider, allow the images in the slider to be clickable and go to specified URL, upload or change images for and create new slides for. The image within the slider must conform to the size of 1024 x 768. Example of deliverable is shown in Appendix 5.1 and Appendix 5.2. The list will allow for the following options:

- *Field Name   Field Type*
- *Title Single line of text*
- *Homepage Image   Hyperlink or Picture*
- *Homepage Description   Multiple lines of text*
- *Active   Yes/No*
- *URL to link to*
- *Hyperlink or Picture*
- *The Title and Homepage Description are option text fields that would appear on the slider.*
- *The active flag is used to determine if the image will appear on the slider. If checked the image should display*
- *URL is an optional field that if populated, the image will link to that URL.*

Non-Functional Requirements

Individual Requirement Details

Req #	Category	Description	Validation	Owner	Comments
4.1.1					
4.1.2					
4.1.3					

Examples of non-functional requirements (*REMEMBER – we want these be as detailed as possible to avoid confusion!!!)

File Types: All file types are allowed with the exception of the list outlined in Appendix 5.3 - SharePoint farm admin

Search Availability: Files are available in search within 30 minutes however there are rare exceptions of up to a 24 hour wait. -N/A

Onboarding process:New users will be added to the site along with the market based libraries (if on does not already exist) - Site Owner: This process / responsibility will be of the site owner.

5.0 Technical (Installation / Deployment) Requirements

Participant	Business Role	Responsibility	Commitment

(Specify the individuals involved with installing and deploying this solution. This section may not be necessary if the solution has a defined Deployment Strategy document.)

Appendix

EXAMPLE - Appendix A: Detailed image of news story page.

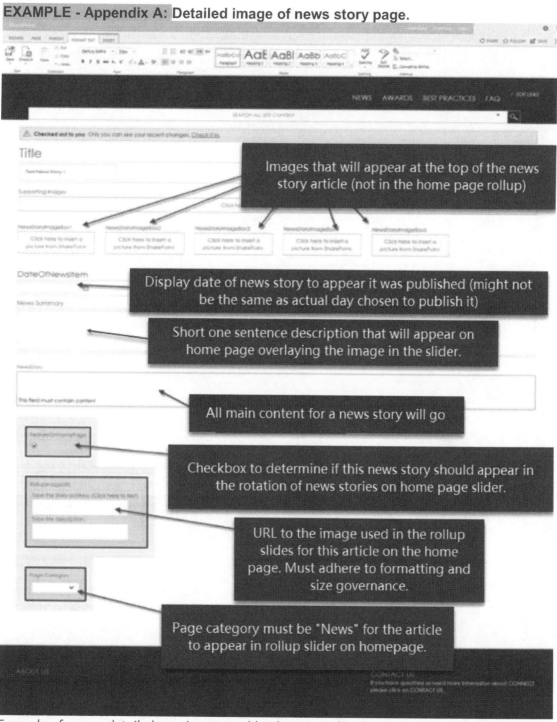

Example of a very detailed requirement addendum regarding how a news story page that will also include the ability to roll up to the home page in SharePoint. The organizations logos and wording has been intentionally removed to protect their identity.

EXAMPLE - Appendix B: Detailed breakdown of homepage functionality.

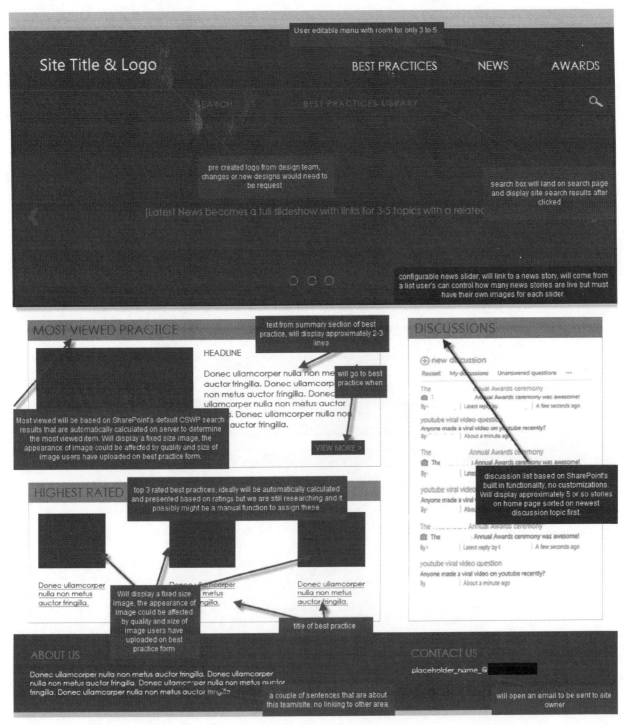

Example of a very detailed requirement addendum regarding how a home page will function in SharePoint. The organizations logos and wording has been intentionally removed to protect their identity.

Example of unsupported file types allowed to be uploaded in SharePoint.

The file extensions blocked by default are shown in the following table.

File Extension	File Type
.ashx	ASP.NET Web handler file. Web handlers are software modules that handle raw HTTP requests received by ASP.NET.
asmx	ASP.NET Web Services source file
asp	Active Server Pages
aspq	Active Server Pages
axd	ASP.NET source file
cshtm	
cshtml	ASP.NET web page (CSHTML)
.json	JavaScript Object Notation file
.rem	Blackberry Encrypted Data file
.shtm	Blackberry Encrypted Data file
.shtm	HTML file that contains server-side directives
.shtml	HTML file that contains server-side directives
.soap	Simple Object Access Protocol file
.stm	HTML file that contains server-side directives
.svc	Windows Communication Foundation (WCF) service file
.vbhtm	ASP.NET Razor web page
.vbhtml	ASP.NET Razor web page
.xamlx	Visual Studio Workflow service file

Example of unsupported file types in SharePoint for uploading.

Approval and Authorization Form

My signature on this form indicates that I am satisfied that this requirements specification is complete and accurate. Changes or deviations from the proposed solution will be submitted via the project's associated Change Management Process.

Name	Signature	Department	Date

PAGE INTENTIONALLY LEFT BLANK

Field Data Type Document

Form Name: Billing Summary List Form

Field Name	Field Type	Field Description (user help)	More Detail	Required
Title	Single line of text			Yes
Summary	Multiple lines of text		Enhanced rich text (Rich text with pictures, tables, and hyperlinks)	Yes
Department	Choice (menu to choose from)			Yes
Department Code	Number (1, 1.0, 100)	Enter the billing code for the department in numbers		Yes
Billing Amount	Currency ($, ¥, €)		Format should be British Pounds	Yes
Date of Bill	Date and Time	The date you want the bill to active		Yes
Project Name	Lookup (information already on this site)		Looks up to project list	Yes
Needs Executive Signoff	Yes/No (check box)	Does this need a C level executive or above approval?		Yes
Billing Representative	Person or Group			No
Link to Project	Hyperlink or Picture	URL to the project site that was built		Yes
Due Date	Calculated (based on other columns)		Add 30 days to Date of Bill field	Yes
Bill Sent	Task			Yes

	Outcome			
External Content Type	External Data		Use the invoice content type	No
Project Tags	Managed Metadata		Use the managed metadata term set for project categories	No

PAGE INTENTIONALLY LEFT BLANK

OFFICE 365 & SHAREPOINT "INTRANET IN A BOX"
BEFORE YOU BUY IT
QUESTIONNAIRE

Purpose, Copyright and Usage

Purpose

This document was created as a questionnaire to empower you to make your own decision on whether or not you should purchase a pre-built intranet for SharePoint or Office 365. Also, if you decide to purchase a pre-built intranet or "intranet in a box" for SharePoint or Office 365, I hope it assists you in making the best decision possible to avoid future issues that could occur without doing proper research. This document was created completely unbiased and I have not been compensated in any way for any opinions in it.

Copyright and Usage

This document is free to use for the evaluation of products in your job role at the company you are working for. Please do not repost it on the internet or share it with others without permission. Also, please do not copy the information and claim it to be your own or include it in literature or "works" for a consulting company you may or may not work for. Other than this, I hope it helps you evaluate the purchase of a pre-built SharePoint/Office 365 "intranet in a box".

SharePoint ™ and Office 365 ™ are trademarks of Microsoft ©

Thank you – Matthew

Why Are You Buying the Product?

- What is your purpose for buying this?
- Are you hoping to cut down on development times and costs?
- Are you hoping to supplement part of your development with this product for more basic requests from your users?
- Are you hoping to create a unified experience across your intranet?
- Would it be easier to let someone else deal with the constant changes that occur in SharePoint & Office 365?
- Are you having trouble finding SharePoint or Office 365 talent to develop the products?
- Have you spent too much money on development and hope to reduce those costs?
- Do you need to be able to deliver solutions to your users much faster?

Whatever your reason is fine, but make sure the cost of doing it yourself is not a better return on ROI than a purchase. Also, make sure the product you are purchasing (or renting) will meet the business needs you have.

Real-World Example

A very large international company I was consulting at wanted to supplement their intranet offerings by purchasing an intranet in a box product to give to their internal customers who had simple website requests. However, the functionality of the products evaluated was limited. The product selected for purchase did not support language translation (variations or machine translation), which for an international company is not ideal. The company had hoped that the vendor would possibly alter their product to accommodate some of their business needs, but the vendor did not seem interested in doing so. However, some of the company's requests were on the vendor's roadmap months away at least. In the end, custom development would have been needed so there was no ROI benefit.

Costs & Licensing

First, get a total all-inclusive price quote from the vendor. They may need more information from you such as approximate numbers of users, numbers of sites or other things, but everyone has a budget. It is good to know before you spend a lot of time and money if the budget is realistic for you.

Other questions to ask include:

- Do you own the code, are you renting it, what happens to the code or sites if you break the relationship with the vendor?
- What happens if the company stops making the product? I have seen two companies already "throw in the towel" as they say and it is unclear what happened to the clients who had purchased the product.
- Cost, per site, per person, annual fees, both, ask for real examples of total usage costs
- Uses – all intranet, hybrid with your own, hybrid with company adding more
- How does the pricing work for the product?
- Is it per user, per farm, per site, or possibly a combination of these?
- Is there an annual maintenance fee?
- Is there a separate cost to "launch" the product as a project at your company?
- Will there be additional costs from spending your own time training users on how to use the product or does the company provide training in some manner on how to use it?

Real-World Example

After spending months evaluating and narrowing down potential products to purchase at a client, it was discovered there was an annual fee and a mandatory project launch fee of around $30,000. Due to the layers of management at this organization, simple questions such as these listed in this blog post and in my free checklist were not asked of the vendor by the client's management. In the end, months of time were lost by myself, the company, the users at the company who needed the website and the vendor selling it.

Company & the Product

Ask for other real customer references who have purchased the product (as with interviewing a job candidate, it is usually a courtesy to only ask for these if a product is in your final selection process).

- How long has the product been in existence and how many versions does it have? If a vendor can say a few years and a few versions, this could be a good sign they are in it for the long haul and have ironed out some bugs.
- How much documentation and literature does the company have on the product? Also, very little documentation could be a sign that the company hasn't spent much time on this product yet.
- Does the company also offer consulting services? Do research on the company itself to see if the company has a good reputation.

SharePoint Specific Questions

- Are there any features, web parts or other things in SharePoint this product won't work with?
- Does the product work with foreign languages (variations / language translations)?
- Will the design apply to different search templates?
- Will simple things such as adding or changing a column on create issues?
- Is the web browser compatibility the same as what SharePoint supports?
- Did the company build their own custom web parts to use instead of the OOTB SharePoint web parts? How do they work, can you test them (see section on insisting on a live demo below)?
- Does the product support managed metadata navigation or have a mega-menu? How is it updated, are there limits to it?
- Are there any issues with different authentication scenarios such as federation, claims or single-sign on that would prevent certain assets of their product loading?
- Are the design files hosted within the SharePoint site assets, style library, a separate site collection or off-site such as CDN network on AWS or Azure?

Real-World Example

Deploying a CSWP (content search web part) will allow you to display results in different ways. Some of the display templates did not work and produced a random GUID error. In another case, there were only a couple of page layout choices and they only had a few columns each. Adding another column to the page layout or content type was not supported. Another issue was that since the My Sites were in a different

Product Support

SharePoint Office 365 intranets are constantly evolving and changing. What are the support and change agreements the vendor is offering for their software?

- If Microsoft comes out with a change that affects their software, what is the turnaround time to come up with an alternate solution or fix?
- What qualifies as a bug, free change and/or fix and what doesn't?
- Is the vendor following the strict branding guidelines on the Microsoft website?
- Will they allow you to customize the site vs. what they give you and will the support change? Are you even allowed to or able to change any of the code?

Real-World Example

Microsoft recently ended support for putting HTML in calculated columns. They also came out with some new, very strict design guidelines regarding placing your own custom design on top of Office 365 which I have clearly seen some vendors not follow. Another item was an intranet product that had all of the design files being hosted on AWS, meaning, you couldn't even touch any of the JavaScript of CSS files to make a change if you wanted to (although an override with on-page JS might have worked,

Design

Does the custom branding that comes with the product spread across all areas within a SharePoint site collection including the following?

1. OOTB and custom lists
2. Document and page libraries
3. Search and search results
4. My sites / user profiles
5. Navigation
6. OOTB web parts (which ones -- there are some that probably can't work entirely with a custom intranet)

- Is the design responsive and will work on most popular mobile devices?
- To what extent will the vendor allow your logo and branding?
- If your purchase consideration is for Office 365, does the template work across the other suite of Office 365 products as well? The branding might not apply, but will integration still work with things such as PowerApps, Flow, Teams, Yammer, etc.?

Roadmap

- Does the company have a roadmap for the product documented to show you?
- Does it align with your needs?
- Does it align with Microsoft's vision for SharePoint & Office 365?

Insist on a Demo in Your Environment

Seeing pretty pictures or a demo via a webinar is one thing, having an actual working sample in your own environment is another. Although there is the viewpoint from the vendor that you could steal their code by implementing a sample site in your environment, I would highly suggest that if a vendor is in your final selection process, you insist upon this step. You may realize many things you had not realized before by doing so. "Touching and using" something is not the same as just seeing it.

Real-World Example

After narrowing down the selection process to one intranet product, a sample demo site was implemented at the client. There were several bugs discovered by actually using it. Things such as mousing over the ribbon bar made the entire screen fly over 10% (probably a CSS float issue) or realizing that lists were not included in the design but page libraries were. Random error messages also appeared frequently. Some bugs were explainable, others required the vendor to fix them.

Alterations & Changes

- To what extent will the vendor let you add your logo branding?
- What custom configurations are already built into the product?
- Are any changes possible and to what extent?
- If changes are allowed, will they only be allowed to be made by the consulting company and what is the cost they will charge you per hour for future changes?
- Is the intranet built on other technologies such as Angular, React, a combination of other things or something else? This is just something to be aware of so you realize what code is running the system depending on what your future plans are and the newer technologies Microsoft is using to build SharePoint.

Usability & Training

- How easy are the instructions for both the admin to install and the end users to use and how detailed are they? Unless the company who built it is offering free training as a part of the purchase, this would mean more hours spent investing in the product you wouldn't normally include in the initial purchase price.

Make sure some your users or stakeholders are involved to see how easy it is to use and if it will meet their requirements.

Conclusion

Once again, I am not saying you should or shouldn't buy one of the pre-built Office 365 / SharePoint intranets out in the marketplace. There are some benefits to being able to offer a professionally designed site to your users with the click of a few buttons. There are also disadvantages of being dependent on one specific consulting company who has built the product for as long as you run your intranet. Possibly, your best solution is a hybrid approach of creating custom sites with the same design as an intranet you purchase (for more complex needs) and using the intranet in a box product for your basic web sites that don't require too much functionality.

Mostly, I want to empower you to make your own decision by knowing as many facts as possible and thinking about possible issues that could happen now instead of later.

As always, if you have any questions, I will try to make time to help or might be available as an independent consultant to assist you. Feel free to contact me at the information below:

Website: http://www.matthewjbailey.com

Email: sharepointmatthew@gmail.com

LinkedIn: http://www.linkedin.com/in/matthewjbailey1

Twitter: @matthewjbailey1

Noteworthy Technology Training: http://www.noteworthytt.com

PAGE INTENTIONALLY LEFT BLANK

Statement of Work

Project Name here

Version:

Status:

Last Updated:

Updated By:

PROJECT TITLE			
COMPANY NAME		CLIENT	
PROJECT MANAGER		DATE SUBMITTED	
PROJECT SPONSOR		VERSION NUMBER	
PROJECT BEGIN DATE		END DATE	

OBJECTIVE	RATIONALE

IN SCOPE	OUT OF SCOPE

REFERENCE DOCUMENTS – NAME	LOCATION & VERSION

DELIVERY APPROACH
The SharePoint Team will carry out work outlined in requirements in the development environmen
SharePoint Team will perform QA and UAT activities.
The Client or client representative will perform user acceptance testing on the solution
The SharePoint Team will work to promote changes into production.

DUE DATE	COMPLETION CRITERIA	DELIVERABLE DESCRIPTION

Estimate Assumptions and Constraints:

This cost is: _____Fixed Bid _____Time & Materials

Annual support contract required: ____Yes ____No

RATE SCHEDULE			
ESTIMATED COST (per hour or task)	PHASE	DELIVERY SCHEDULE	DESCRIPTION
$500			
$200			
$75 per hr			
10% of project cost	Project	ongoing	Annual support costs and licensing

SUPPORT CONSTRAINT
The scope of this Statement of Work for support includes up to _____ hours of annual support beginning _____ (_____ hours total). Support hours will expire _____ and can / cannot be carried over to the following year. The SharePoint team will renew options for support in _____ within _____ days of expiration.

Total Project Fixed Cost: $

Ongoing Annual Costs (if applicable): $

Customer Acceptance:

When initial design and development is completed, a copy will be delivered for review by the project sponsor. Based on the customer's acceptance, the process to begin development will begin. Acceptance and sign off of the above delivery approach will determine customer acceptance. The project sponsor team will return the signed acceptance form(s) or declare their refusal of all or any part of the document after reviewing the delivery of product in an agreed upon timeframe. After that time, acceptance will be assumed and billing processed accordingly.

_____	_____	_____
Project Sponsor	Date	GL/Project/Account/Depart. Number

_____ _____

Business Analyst or Project Manager   Date

THIS PAGE INTENTIONALLY LEFT BLANK

_____Project

Provider Hosted Add-in (app) Architecture Proposal

Version:

Status:

Last Updated:

Updated By:

1.0 Overview

A provider hosted app is a self-enclosed program running on a server outside of the SharePoint environment (usually a completely different server). It allows one to write code in many different languages that can connect, read, write and interact with data from SharePoint when deployed to SharePoint.

1.1 Advantages

1.1.1 Security

The application is secure because the reading and writing is happening on the server, not via client side coding and would not have endpoints for client-side scripting open to hack into via JavaScript.

1.1.2 Performance

Because the server is doing the processing in compiled code, there would not be a noticeable delay for each user using the program as there would be with InfoPath due to its need to evaluate formulas to hide and display fields.

1.2 Disadvantages

1.2.1 Governance

Could be an issue to create if the organization has governance issues with allowing apps to be installed into the app catalog.

1.2.2 Key Expiration

A key issued by Microsoft is only good for 2 years. If after this time the app would still be needed, a new key would need to be requested and added to the app, then re-uploaded. This would take about 10 minutes to accomplish for a developer.

2.0 Architecture

2.1 System Architecture

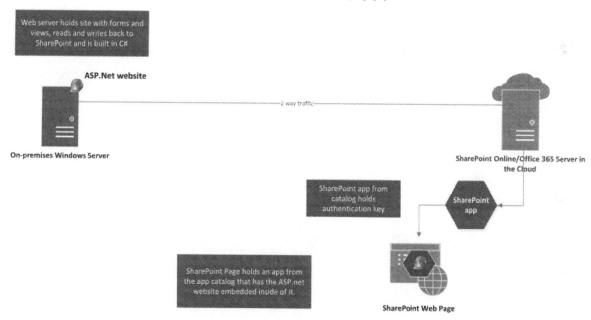

Provider Hosted Add-In (app) Architecture

3. Build Process

1. Building an ASP.net site using web forms or MVC in Visual Studio with C# utilizing OAuth to authenticate to SharePoint

2. Building a low-trust add-in (app) that only holds a secret token to allow authentication to allow the ASP.net site to authenticate to SharePoint, this also might have to include code to hide the app from other sites unless there is not a concern of who sees it (as it wouldn't work on another site collection unless we programmed it do so)

3. Creating the main list to hold all of the records in SharePoint

4. Creating PowerShell scripts running on scheduled tasks to handle the data import from Excel into SharePoint / sending emails possibly date assignment routine *(*Note: the same timeout/network errors are still a possible concern)*

5. Possibly one or two SharePoint Designer workflows, most "workflow" like coding would take place in the ASP.net site listed in item 1.

6. SharePoint security groups created with a custom permission inside SharePoint site collection

7. Date assignment code would run either via a list or page outside of the add-in (app)

4. Installation

4.1 Installation Process

1. An ASP.net site would need to be deployed to a server running IIS

2. An app would need to be deployed to the App Catalog in SharePoint (although only to hold a key for authentication, it would not be like the other apps in the catalog that are filled with code)

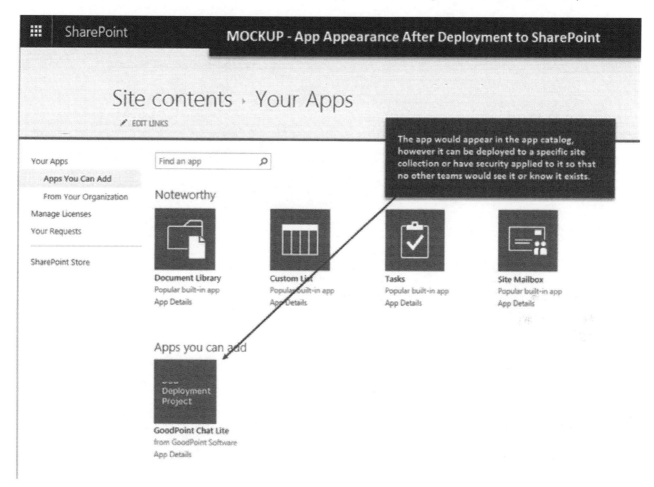

3. The app would be added to a SharePoint page

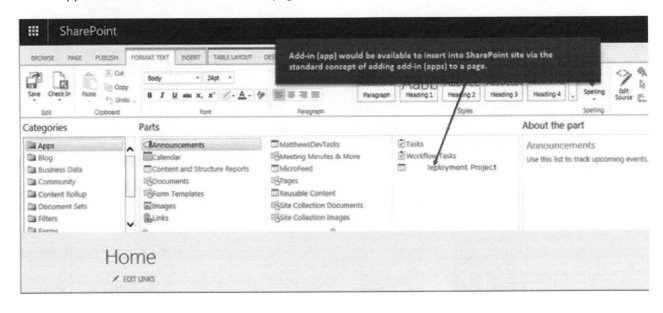

THIS PAGE LEFT INTENTIONALLY BLANK

ABOUT THE AUTHOR

Matthew J. Bailey is a is a Microsoft Certified Trainer for Noteworthy Technology Training specializing in SharePoint, Office 365, Azure & Power BI. He is certified as a MCT, MCSE, MCP & MCSA. Utilizing a mixture of consulting experience at major corporations with teaching, he loves to share skills learned as a SharePoint business analyst, administrator, trainer & developer obtained from over 10 years of working with Microsoft technologies. He enjoys speaking at conferences, from Ignite to local community events and user groups. He is also an avid blogger and author.

You can learn more about him by visiting his website at http://www.matthewjbailey.com

Made in the USA
Middletown, DE
02 June 2018